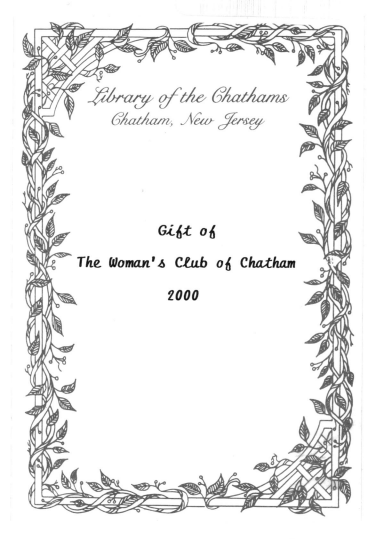

TANGLED LIVES

Tangled Lives

Daughters, Mothers,
and the Crucible of Aging

LILLIAN B. RUBIN

Beacon Press

BOSTON

Beacon Press
25 Beacon Street
Boston, Massachusetts 02108-2892
www.beacon.org

Beacon Press books
are published under the auspices of
the Unitarian Universalist Association of Congregations.

05 04 03 02 01 00   8 7 6 5 4 3 2 1

This book is printed on acid-free paper that meets the uncoated paper
ANSI/NISO specifications for permanence as revised in 1992.

Text design by Elizabeth Elsas
Composition by Wilsted & Taylor Publishing Services

Library of Congress Cataloging-in-Publication Data
   Rubin, Lillian B.
     Tangled lives : daughters, mothers, and the crucible of aging /
   Lillian B. Rubin.
       p.   cm.
     ISBN 0-8070-6794-6
     1. Mothers and daughters.   2. Parent and adult child.   I. Title.
   HQ755.86 .R83   2000
   306.874'3—dc21

                                                    00-008458

FOR MARCI,
THE DAUGHTER WHO LIGHTS MY LIFE

It was about ten years ago. We were sitting in my living room—my mother, my daughter, myself—when Marci, my daughter, took each of us by the hand and pulled us forward to face the full-length mirror on the wall. "Look, Grandma," my forty-year-old daughter urged my eighty-five-year-old mother. "Look at us, three generations of strong women."

It was the first time in years we had all been together, and I stood staring at our reflections, watching my mother's usually unyielding mien soften a bit in the face of her granddaughter's enthusiasm; feeling grateful for my daughter's determined attempt to turn a difficult visit with my mother into something more satisfying; and captured by a tableau that revealed so sharply such differing aspects of my self—the self I was as my mother's daughter, the woman I've become as my daughter's mother.

My eyes saw our faces in the mirror but my mind burst with images from the past, memories of me as daughter and mother, of them as mother and daughter; snapshots of moments and events that brought us from there to here. It was a powerful vision in which I saw myself refracted through my roles as daughter, as mother, as child, as woman—and looked also into the face of my own old age.

I knew then that one day I would write this book. But it took my mother's death and my own struggle with finding myself at the head of the generational line in this, the seventh decade of my life, to be able to write the story I saw reflected in that mirror—the story of my relationships with my mother and my daughter, the tales of the past mingling with my struggle in the present as I search for a way to live with the uncertain future aging brings.

As I stand in the doorway to this next stage of my life, it seems fitting to look back—back to a past that will explain me more fully to myself, to reflect on the paths, the choices, the people, the accidents of life that brought me here—an inquiry that, I hope, will help me chart the course to the future. For this is a revolutionary moment in the history of human life, the first time most of us will live long enough to see old age and be healthy enough to enjoy it. Those of us who stand on the threshold of this new old age, and those who will soon come to it, are looking into uncharted territory—years that open opportunities for living that were unknown to earlier generations along with plenty of anxiety about how we'll find our way through them.

I know no more about how to do that than anyone else. But I do know how to engage the inquiry, how to look at the issues—those that are my own and those that have a more universal resonance—open them up, examine them, feel them, come to terms with them. This book is about that struggle—an exploration that, I hope, will help others find their own way into and out of it.

Chapter One

"Damn, when do I get to be old?" I think resentfully as I drag myself out of bed just after dawn. It's one of those beautiful San Francisco mornings when a billowy fog bank hangs over the ocean, its lacy tendrils creating magical forms as they spill over the Golden Gate Bridge. But I have no time to linger.

Forty-five minutes later I'm hurtling down the freeway in a taxi, heading for the airport to catch the eight o'clock flight to Miami, where my ninety-four-year-old mother has been in a nursing home for the last year. I look out at the bay, the water cool and green in the morning light, and brood, "I'm too old for this, too tired. These trips take too much out of my aging body, not to mention what they do to my psyche."

Twenty years ago, it was fifty-year-old "children" taking care of their seventy-year-old parents; now it's seventy-year-olds looking after their ninety-something elders. Last Sunday the *New York Times* did a story on "assisted living" places for the aged that featured a photograph of a daughter helping her mother get settled in one of them. I couldn't tell without reading the caption who was the mother, who the daughter.

At the gate, I hand over my ticket in return for a boarding pass and prepare to wait. I've lost count of how many of these trips I've made this year, four or five maybe. My husband and daughter keep asking why I go. "She doesn't recognize you anymore," they argue, "and even when she did, it didn't make any difference to her. All she wants is your brother, and he's dead."

They're right; my relationship with my mother has been troubled since I was a very small child, and my being there now doesn't seem to offer her much comfort or consolation. Yet I go, not so much for her but for me—for the child inside who still hopes for something, not approval exactly, but some way to define the relationship more positively; and for the adult who knows she has to do it "right" now to avoid guilt later.

The plane is due into Miami at 5:30 in the afternoon, too late, I tell myself, to go to see my mother. It's not too late, of course, but it's the excuse I need to have dinner with a friend. He's my gift to myself whenever I make this journey—a long, leisurely, lovely dinner among the young and the beautiful who inhabit Miami's South Beach, my antidote to the absurdity of life and death in a nursing home.

The next morning, I dawdle over breakfast, putting off my visit as long as conscience allows. It isn't just seeing my mother that's so difficult; it's the whole atmosphere: the sights, the sounds, the smells. Worst of all is the confrontation with my future. At seventy-three it's impossible to be here without asking, "Is this what's in store for me?" I shudder and tell myself that I'll never let it happen, that I'll take my life before I live this indignity. Brave words. But can we ever know what we'll do when the moment is upon us?

Finally, I enter the building, check in at the front desk, and take the elevator to my mother's third-floor room. As I step into the corridor, I'm greeted by five wheelchairs facing the elevators expectantly. For a moment, my mind trips out on an image of the chairs gliding off by themselves into some adventure. In reality, the chairs are occupied by three women and two men, all clearly living in some other universe in their minds. Their bodies, slumped in the chairs, are so limp they seem to have no bones. One woman mumbles incoherently, a nonstop rhythmic set of sounds that no one understands; a man's palsied hands shake uncontrollably; the others sit quietly, their eyes closed, their heads lying lopsided on their shoulders as if the muscles and tendons that used to hold them in place have worn out.

"What are they doing here?" I ask an attendant at the nurses station nearby.

"It's recreation time," she replies cheerily. "They're waiting to go down to the rec room." *Recreation time! Am I crazy, or are they?*

The scene at the elevator and the explanation follow me as I make my way down the hall to my mother's room. When I came to make the arrangements to move my mother into this place, I was impressed when the director showed me around and outlined all the activities available for residents. Now I wonder fretfully whether I blinded myself to the reality that these "activities" are little more than a bureaucratic response to state licensing requirements. But perhaps I'm being uncharitable. It's possible, too, that this pretense that some semblance of normal life exists here is the only way the staff can cope with the incongruity of dealing with the living dead.

I enter my mother's room preoccupied with the realization that if I had allowed myself to "see" then what is so obvious now, I might have been forced to look for another solution. But what would it have been? My mother couldn't live alone, nor was the euphemistically named "family residential center" in which she had resided for two years able to continue to care for her. It was a nursing home or my home, and that I couldn't do. I flinch when I see those words staring back at me, fearful that the world out there will know me for the selfish daughter my mother always said I was.

My attention is diverted by my mother's new roommate. She's younger than most of the people here and seems fully competent as she sits up in her chair, a tray table in front of her. "I'm Pat," she says, her right hand patting her chest as she speaks. "I can't walk."

I smile, say a few of words of greeting, and turn to my mother who lies still and frail in her bed. "Hi, Mom," I say.

Her eyes flicker open and look at me vacantly. "Mom, it's me, Lillian, your daughter."

She turns away, mumbling, "I have no daughter; she died."

"No," I insist, even as I understand the folly of my attempt to penetrate her fog, "I'm here, right here."

She rouses herself, looks at me with a brief flash of recognition, then sinks back into the pillow and mumbles in Yiddish, "*Gottenyu,* why did you take my son and leave her? It's him I need, not her."

I've heard these words often since my brother Leonard's death (Len, we called him as an adult, Lenny when he was a child), but they still jab at my soul. I sigh, caught, as I have been for so many years, between my hurt and anger (What kind of mother thinks such things, let alone says them?) and my struggle to understand this woman who birthed me. I remind myself that it was Len, not I, who never moved very far from my mother's side. Never mind that he suffered his own love-hate ambivalence about her, or that their relationship was marked by often cruel and hateful fights. He was emotionally, even symbiotically, linked to my mother in ways that I was not—not even when I was a child. Who knows who was at fault? I've often thought we were simply mismatched—a mother and a child who shouldn't have had to live in the same family. What I do know is that when my brother moved from New York to Florida a few years before he died, he couldn't rest until he brought her there as well. I left for California nearly fifty years ago and never looked back.

I'm relieved to be distracted from my thoughts by Pat, who keeps thumping her chest noisily and repeating, "I'm Pat, I can't walk"—a mantra meant perhaps to remind herself that she's still a person. "Maybe if I talk to her, she'll settle down," I think. But there is no conversation; she has no other words, at least none she's willing or able to share with me.

I sit at my mother's bedside, Pat's words like a soft drumbeat in the background, and feel the anger rising inside me. My mother is dying, yet she won't give an inch. If I were my own patient in therapy, I'd ask, "So why would you think it would be different now?" I don't think so, but I can't help wishing it were so.

It's hard seeing this woman, once so all-powerful in my life — the person I feared, hated, loved — now lying helpless before me. It isn't that I want her to live; rather it's nearly intolerable to see her so diminished, so demeaned. She was so tough, so fiercely independent, so unyielding. Now here she is, broken, her mind wandering in and out of a reality that seems to me insufferable, kicking, clawing, biting, cursing at the attendants who come to clean her up. *To change her diapers.* The image is blinding, incomprehensible. My indomitable mother, a woman for whom control seemed to equal survival, now suffers the ultimate loss of control. Who wouldn't want to kick and scream, to curse the helper instead of the God who abandoned her to this living death?

I, too, want to scream my protest, "This isn't a fitting end to her life." Or to mine. It's impossible to sit here without conjuring with my own demons about aging, without confronting my own pained understanding that I'm not far behind.

Anita, my mother's attendant for the day, interrupts my thoughts. "You're her daughter, huh?" she asks as she comes into the room. "She's tough, your mama; she don't do nothing she don't want to do."

On the inside I think angrily, "Boy, don't I know that." Outside I shrug my assent wordlessly.

Anita turns toward the bed and shouts, "It's time to get dressed, Rae." No answer. Impatient, she shouts louder, "Rae, did you hear me, Rae. It's time to get dressed."

"Why doesn't anyone here talk to these patients in a normal tone of voice?" I think irritably. Aloud, I say, "She's not deaf; you don't have to shout so loudly."

"Well," she says, vexed at the perceived criticism, "you can't always tell."

But it isn't only an inability to "tell" that makes people shout at the old. It has to do also with our cultural assumptions about the aged, with the deeply held, if unarticulated belief, that the aged are also infirm, not just physically but mentally. So we shout because we feel helpless in the face of infirmity, because somehow shouting seems to give more force to our words, to offer more hope that we'll be heard and understood. Even more discomfiting, the old are a mirror on our future, a terrifying image that threatens our denial of our own mortality, one from which we turn in angry disgust as we try to shout it down.

After a brief struggle, Anita gets my mother dressed and into a wheelchair while I prepare to take her for a walk by the beach. We walk in the warm sunshine until it's time for lunch, which, I remember from previous visits, is served in what they call the recreation room. When we arrive there, I see a semicircle of wheelchairs, all occupied by people like those who greeted me at the elevator. Inside the circle an attendant sits beside a portable stereo that's playing music so loud that those in the room who are still competent are covering their ears.

I settle my mother in a corner as far from the music as I can get, but neither thought nor conversation are possible in the din. Unable to stand the noise for very long, I go up to the aide, tap her on the shoulder to get her attention, and shout, "The music is much too loud, can you turn it down, please."

She looks at me offended, draws herself up to her full height, and says, her sweeping gesture taking in the near comatose people around her. "I can't turn it down; this is their music lesson." Then, as I stand there wide-eyed, wondering if I've entered a loony bin instead of an old-age home, she says, as if it explains this bizarre scene, "We do it every day at this time."

I cross the room to where my mother sits, thinking, "Maybe it does explain it." Not the music lesson, but the attendant's prideful response. We all do it in one way or another. We make sense out of senseless events by imbuing them with meaning. It's God's will; it's nature's way; it's fate, kismet—anything that allows us to avoid confronting the inexplicable, the mysterious, the randomness of so many of life's events.

For this woman, as for others who work in nursing homes, life on the job is filled with the senseless, for the senselessness of both life and death is particularly acute in this setting. It's easier to come to work every day if she can make herself believe that she's doing something useful, that her activities here have some meaning. So when she gathers her charges together, she's not just surrounded with people who long ago lost consciousness, she's bringing them pleasure with her music lesson. Who's to say she isn't? I muse as I take a seat next to my mother. Do I know any better than she what's going on in their heads and hearts? I shake my head, impatient with my thoughts. Am I, too, determined to make sense out of the senseless?

My mother refuses to eat any lunch, so I take her back upstairs. I sit at her bedside, Pat's unending mantra providing the background music to my thoughts, when a woman wanders into the room, plops down on my lap, and puts a finger in her mouth. She's a small person, dressed in a kind of clown's outfit—brilliant green shirt, hot pink skirt, harlequin stockings, and no shoes. My astonishment strikes me dumb for a moment, then I gently stand both of us up and say, "Hello, what's your name?" She beams, with a brilliant smile that lights up her face, and replies with an incomprehensible stream of sounds. She's young looking, middle fifties, I imagine, too young to fit my classic image of the Alzheimer's patient.

I don't know if I've made contact with her, but she seems perfectly happy to be babbling at me. Not knowing what else to do, I sit down again and so does she, taking her place once more on my lap. Soon an attendant comes looking for her, "You can't stay here, Lita; you know that," she scolds. Then, as she takes her by the hand to lead her down the hall to her own room, the attendant turns to me. "She wanders," she says apologetically.

But wandering Lita won't stay put. So we replay the same scene repeatedly through the afternoon as she comes for the comfort of my lap and the attendant comes to take her away.

"Let her stay," I finally say, "she's not doing any harm."

"I can't," the attendant replies. "It's against the rules."

"What rule says a patient can't find comfort somewhere; I don't mind if she's here."

But the rules say no and there's no give.

I sit there angrily, thinking of the time when my mother fell out of bed and broke her hip two days after she'd been admitted here. "Why weren't the rails up on her bed during the night," I demanded to know.

"The state of Florida has a rule against any restraints," explained the director.

"Even when it jeopardizes the health and safety of the patients?" I asked, incredulous.

"Yes, if an inspector came and saw the rails up on the beds, we'd lose our triple A rating."

It's easy to understand the thinking behind the rules. Nursing homes have been known to abuse their patients with unnecessary restraints—physical, chemical, or both. But as with so many rules that are designed to correct such problems, their bureaucratic application often creates new difficulties, sometimes as bad as the ones they sought to cure.

Now that Lita is gone, my attention turns to a man, probably in his late seventies, who, with one foot, has been propelling his wheelchair up and down the hall. Up and back he goes, each rhythmic energetic push scooting him along at an impressive pace. What does this journey to nowhere mean to him?

I move toward the hall and watch from the doorway. After a few trips, he stops before me and, his voice edged with hostility, asks, "What're you looking at?"

"You," I reply. "I can't help wondering why you do that all day."

"What would you do if you were in this crazy place?"

The question pulls me up short as I search for an answer. Reluctantly, I finally say, "I don't know; maybe I'd read a book."

"I can't do that; it's too hard to concentrate on anything here," he counters.

"You look and sound pretty good to me. What are you doing here anyway?" I ask.

"What am I doing here?" he snorts, a bitter anger suffusing his features. "What am I doing here? Ask my damn kids. They'll tell you. I had this stroke, and as soon as I couldn't take care of myself like they thought I should, they shoved me in here, threw me away like a piece of garbage."

I shudder, thinking, "That's what my mother said when I brought her here." Almost before the thought is fully formed, I reassure myself, "But she needed to be here; she couldn't take care of herself anymore." Words that don't still my guilt which asks, "Is

that what we 'children' always tell ourselves? Is that what we need
to believe so we can live with the choices we make?"

I turn back to my mother and leave the man to his frantic pacing. The day is gone, and by now I feel as if I'll go mad if I don't get
out of here. I'll be back tomorrow morning for a couple of hours
before I have to catch my noon flight to San Francisco. But right
now it's time to leave.

I walk the mile or so to my hotel, enjoying the balmy evening
air of Miami that's so unlike the chill that descends on San Francisco as soon as the sun goes down. South Beach is alive with people and, as the restaurants and clubs turn their sound systems up to
attract attention, the music of Cuba spills out on to the street. I'm
restless, feeling at odds with myself, and know I'll have trouble settling down in my hotel room. So I stop at one of the sidewalk cafés
to watch the action and sip some wine. I tell myself I should eat
something; I've had nothing since my bagel and tea at breakfast. I
order a seafood salad, but my stomach rebels, and I can do little
more than pick at it indifferently. An hour or more passes; the
crowds grow thicker, the noise louder. It's time for me to leave.

Back in my hotel room, I pick up the novel that held my attention all the way across the country. Now I find myself reading the
same paragraph over and over without comprehension. I dig
around in my suitcase and find the mystery I brought with me as
well, thinking I can always get into one of those. But I don't do
any better with Patricia Cornwell than I did with Charles Frazier's
Civil War tale. I flip on the TV and watch some inane program in
the hope that it will put me to sleep. It doesn't.

I spend a long, restless night, dozing off and being jolted awake
repeatedly by unpleasant dreams I can't remember. I'm relieved
when I finally see daylight peeking through the spaces in the
blackout curtains on my windows. I dress, pack up my things, and
go out for a long walk before breakfast. Afterward, I pick up my
small suitcase and take a cab to the nursing home.

My mother is still in bed when I arrive, so I help her nurse dress
her, put her in the wheelchair, and push her down to the beach
where we sit in the sun listening to the gulls squawk and relaxing

into the hypnotically rhythmic sight and sound of the ocean as the tides do their work. I talk to my mother, looking for something I know isn't there, but trying anyhow. I don't want a lot; I'm not hoping for some rapprochement that will heal the pain of the past, just some connection however small, some last gift I can give her, take from her, so that the end won't feel so empty. But there's nothing there, at least not for me. Her only comprehensible words are the mantra she repeats every time she becomes aware of my presence. "*Gottenyu,* why did you have to take him and leave her?"

It's time to go, not because I have a plane to catch, but because there's nothing left here for me. It will be easier to wait at the airport than to mark time punishing myself with the pretense that we're having a visit.

I wrestle the wheelchair up a slight rise and finally get my mother back to her room. When she's resettled in bed, I lean over and kiss her dry, weathered cheek. "I have to leave," I say into her ear.

She turns away and so do I. It's the same in death as it has been in life. We have always turned away from each other, my mother and I, always since I was a small child.

I collect my things, reach out to stroke her hair one last time but let my hand fall away instead. *I don't want to touch her!* Outside I hail a cab, sit back, and expect to be flooded with relief at the prospect of being home in a few hours. Instead, I begin to weep, quietly at first, then in big gulping sobs.

"Anything I can do for you, lady?" the cabdriver asks, looking anxiously in the mirror.

But there's nothing anyone can do. I know I've said my last good-bye to my mother—a farewell that was as painful and unsatisfying as our lifetime of hellos have been.

Chapter Two

I sit in the economy section of the plane, more cramped than usual because, as soon as the seat belt sign is turned off, the man in front of me pushes his seat back as far as it will go and keeps it there during the whole flight. Annoyed with myself, I think once again that I ought to fly business class on these long trips. I can afford it, and if I don't want to spend the money, I have plenty of airline frequent flier miles. But although I have no trouble spending money on many other things, the poor little girl who lives inside and still worries about being old and poor, draws the line at such luxuries. It's absurd, I know: I'm already old and it's highly unlikely I'll ever be poor again. But on this one, the past refuses to loosen its hold.

After a seemingly endless, brooding flight, the plane finally touches down in San Francisco and tears of gratitude replace the edginess that dominated my spirit during the whole of my visit with my mother. I'm home! Back to my family, my friends, my work, my life. *My life*—a life that's far more distant from my mother's than the three thousand geographic miles that have separated us for nearly fifty years.

I'm the first one out of my seat when the plane pulls up to the gate, and I wait, dancing impatiently from one foot to the other, as others take their time in gathering their belongings and moving out. As I hurry up the ramp, I see my husband, Hank, whose welcoming smile warms me. Then, as I get closer, my heart compresses when, after these few days away from him, I see more clearly than ever the signs of his aging. His eightieth birthday is just months ahead, a milestone in living that's never far from my mind.

I keep trying to console myself with reminders that it's only another day on the calendar, that he'll be the same man the day after his eightieth birthday as he was the day before, that my anticipatory angst will all have been in vain. But my heart can't hear the words. I'm caught instead by the knowledge that, as the life span continues to increase, gerontologists and demographers have taken to distinguishing between the "young old" and the "old old." At eighty, there's no doubt about where he belongs.

I move quietly, naturally, into his arms, unable to stanch the sudden flow of tears. But I don't know if I'm crying because my mother is dying or because I fear that he will. We've been married for thirty-five years—my second, his third—wonderful years during which dreams I never even had came true. "Stop it!" I tell myself as he holds me tight; "he's healthier than you are." But the shadow of death seems to envelop me, and sadness lives in my soul.

I have hardly eaten anything for two days, and I'm suddenly hungry, so we stop for a bite. We talk, sharing the news of the days apart, the kind of easy conversation of people who have spent half a lifetime together. I know he saw our daughter last night, so I ask, "Anything new with Marci?"

"No, we had a lovely dinner together," he replies, his face wreathed in a smile as he recollects the evening, then fills me in on the details he heard about her recent promotion. She's a successful attorney who, a week or so ago, was appointed senior vice president of the large corporation for which she has worked for some years. I listen, but much as I love and am proud of my daughter, my mind wanders.

"She's dying," I say, "and I feel terrible."

"Because she's dying or because of the life she lived?" he asks.

"Both—and more. But I don't know what. I just know that I didn't expect to feel so sad."

He's silent. After years of hearing my anger at my mother, after all the times he has himself been appalled at her behavior, he doesn't know what to say. So he reaches over and takes my hand, hoping I'll find comfort in his touch. I know what he's thinking, though. "You don't understand why I'm not glad to see her go, do you?"

He demurs. "No, I think I understand, but I guess I wish you could be glad that you soon won't have to deal with her."

It's my turn to be silent, to deal with the jumble of thoughts in my head. Each time I've come home from one of these trips, I felt exhausted and depleted, wondering always why I continued to go, wishing she would die. But until now she held on to life so tenaciously that I nearly convinced myself it would never happen. A child's prophecy, perhaps, since we never wholly give up the vision of the all-powerful parent. Nevertheless, the adult at least half believed it. "She's never going to give me the gift of one day on this earth without her," I'd complain as I stormed around the house after a particularly difficult visit with her.

After a few moments with my thoughts, I return to the conversation. "Don't worry; I'll be okay, but not right now."

By we time we get home night has begun to fall, and the shimmering lights of the western half of the city are spread before me as we walk into our apartment. I stand before the windows, Hank's arm around my shoulder, looking at the view—the blinking reds, greens, and blues of neon, the lights etching the contours of the roadway of the Golden Gate Bridge, the cars and buses that seem to scurry along like ants with headlights, the brilliantly lit cathedral at the University of San Francisco, the stars luminous against the dark, navy blue sky. "It's enough to make you believe in God," I murmur to Hank, who tightens his arm around me and says, "Not quite."

The ringing phone shatters the quiet. It's Marci checking in, wanting to know how my trip was, how I am, how her grandmother is doing. Her relationship with my mother has always been distant, partly, no doubt, because mine has been, but also because, being my daughter, she wasn't exempt from my mother's censure. "She's just like you," my mother would complain in a tone that left no doubt about her meaning.

Marci and I talk for a while; I can hear the concern in her voice as I fill her in. "I worry about you, Mom; are you going to be okay?"

I reassure her through my tears. But this time they're tears of gratitude that I have fulfilled the most important mission of my life. I have raised a daughter who is also my friend, an adult child whom I adore and who welcomes me into her life as fully as mine is open to her. She'll never be caught in the kind of ambivalence I feel about my mother's impending death, waiting for her to die, wishing she would, wanting something before she's gone, a word, a gesture, while knowing I won't get it, guilty about my thoughts, wondering how I will feel when it actually happens. I know my daughter will suffer a profound loss when I die, but she'll have the memories of the love we shared to sustain her and the knowledge that she filled my life with joy and pride as well. All I will have are sadness and regret for what wasn't.

The phone keeps ringing. Friends who have lived with me through these trips for the last three years call to say hello, to remind me that they're there if I need them. I talk with Kim for a long time. Until about six weeks ago, she, too, had a mother in a nursing home, a mother with whom she also suffered a difficult relationship. For years we raged to each other about our mothers, regaling each other with stories about the latest atrocity, each helping the other in the struggle to understand these women who so profoundly colored our lives, examining together what part we played in sustaining the antagonisms. Now as we speak, I think about the relief I felt for her when she called to tell me that her mother died. Relief and envy.

I have other very close friends, women and men I love and with whom I've shared intensely intimate relationships for decades. But it's with Kim that I've found the greatest freedom to speak my deepest and least acceptable feelings about my mother. We two have met regularly, perhaps once a month, for many years, usually for a a long walk and lunch or dinner during which we talk about our work, our children, our relationships, ourselves, and, increasingly in recent years, about our mothers' imminent ends—

a conversation in which we give each other permission to think the unthinkable, speak the unspeakable. "I wouldn't dare say these things to anyone else," we say to each other as prohibitions fall away and forbidden thoughts become words.

Often, as we walk along telling each other yet another "bad mother" story, re-creating our fantasies of pleasure in our mother's death, we become convulsed with laughter loud enough to turn heads on the street. It isn't that we're saying anything so funny; rather our laughter is an expression of the uneasiness we feel at daring to speak the forbidden, the kind of nervous laughter of children who whisper dirty words to each other and are titillated by their boldness. Several times when, in a restaurant or coffee shop, we've been laughing wildly at our macabre talk a waiter has commented on how much fun we're having and asks what we're talking about. Our eyes fall to the table when we hear the question; we know if we look at each other we'll erupt into near hysteria. How can we say that we're relishing fantasies about our mothers' deaths? Now, as I tell her my latest mother story, we turn my account of the nursing home—wandering Lita, the music lesson—into laughter, and my dark moodiness lifts by the time we hang up.

It's time to get at the clutter that awaits me at my desk. I check my phone messages, answering those that require immediate attention, then go through both the real and cybermail. I'm always amazed at how much accumulates in just a few days' absence, and irritated with how much of it is junk: solicitations, advertisements, catalogs. As I toss one after the other into the wastebasket, I think once again that when the end comes, the world is more likely to be buried in paper than blown apart by a bomb.

I awaken at six the next morning, eager to get back to my daily life. I will see five therapy patients today and do the two interviews that will complete the research for my study of midlife families. I wonder for the hundredth time why I'm planning to write about middle age when the issues of old age haunt my own life. If, when I began this study, I thought it would help distance me from my own preoccupations, it has been a failure. As I climb out of bed, I shake myself free of these thoughts, "Stop it! You have a contract for the midlife book and you'll do it."

The next two weeks go by quickly as the ordinary demands of my life take over my thoughts. Then on Saturday morning, when I'm lying in bed, my body awake but my mind in that pleasant haze before full consciousness returns, the phone startles me out my reverie. It's my unlisted number which, at this early hour, suggests that it's not good news. I pick it up to hear the unmistakable Spanish-accented voice of my mother's nurse. "Your mother is running a fever," she says, "and the doctor wants to know if you want her treated." I had left explicit orders saying "no treatment" but now, faced with the question, I gulp nervously. I turn to my husband and tell him the news. He shakes his head wordlessly. Finally, I eke out the word *no.*

The next morning, Sunday, Hank and I are in the kitchen beginning the preparations for our Christmas dinner the next day. There will be twelve of us: our daughter, Marci, and Larry, the man she calls her "forever after"; Blake, our grandson; and some of the friends who are part of the surrogate family I've built over many years. Fictive kin, the anthropologists call such relationships. But there's nothing fictional about them. These are the relationships that nurture the soul, friendships that have enriched my life, nourished my heart and mind, and healed some of the hurts sustained in the troubled family of my birth.

The ringing phone jars me, claiming my attention from thoughts of Christmas, friends, and the tart shell I'm rolling out. A chill passes through my body as I lift the receiver to hear, "Lillian, I'm sorry to tell you that your mother passed away this morning." My eyes move to the clock on the wall; it's 9:45. *My mother is dead!* I stand there dumbly, staring at the clock, the phone still at my ear. Why do we look at the clock at such moments? What difference does it make what time it is?

My heart seems to stand still and, for a moment, my mind refuses to comprehend. Then as thought and feeling collide, the tears come—a painful, wrenching sadness that overcomes the relief that lies right next to it. Hank, who has lived with me through decades of on-again, off-again angst over my mother, heaves a sigh of relief. "It's over," he says gently. But I can only stand there weeping as he folds me into his arms. My lifetime adversary—the mother I once loved even as I hated and feared her, the mother with whom I both identified and *dis*identified, who for good and ill marked my life more than any other—is dead.

Chapter Three

As far back as I can remember, my relationship with my mother has been filled with conflict and acrimony. She was an angry, unhappy woman, and I was clearly not the daughter she wanted. Although it's hard to imagine what kind of girl-child could have pleased her. My brother came closer, not for any particular qualities he had, but just because he was a boy. But a girl, well, "Girls shouldn't be born!" was one of the refrains that dominated my childhood.

When I think about those words now, I can believe that, whatever else she meant, they were also a comment on the lot of women, on the hardships of her own life, on what she saw in store for me. Perhaps like many African-American families who try to harden their sons for the life they'll face with discipline that seems harsh to an outsider, my mother was getting me ready for the difficulties of a woman's life. But as a child I'd hear those words—"Girls shouldn't be born!"—and all I could think was that she hated my presence.

So why am I not relieved at the news of her death? The pain I feel seems old, primitive, as if from another time and place. A child's sorrow—the same terrible sadness I felt when, as a five-year-old, I stood and cried as my father's coffin was lowered into his grave. But it isn't only death that evokes these feelings, it's the memory of a life. I'm assaulted with memories of the loneliness and heartache I suffered in my mother's house, of her displeasure and disapproval that were tattooed on my body and my soul. I feel once again the pain of living in a family where I didn't fit, where I might as well have been, as a man I know once said, a dog growing up in a cat family.

I search almost desperately for some good memories. There were moments of kindness, moments when a smile lit her face, even moments of love. I know there were. So why can't I remember them now when I need them? Maybe later. Now I can only weep—for my mother, for myself, for what we never had, now never will have.

One of the things about death, though, is that it calls you into action. There are things to do, funeral arrangements to consider, people to notify, plans to be canceled, new ones to be made. I call my daughter who lives on the other side of San Francisco Bay. "Grandma died," I say through my tears. "Are you okay?" she asks anxiously. Then before I can answer, "I'll be right over."

I hang up and call my brother's first wife from whom he was divorced many years ago. Although he remarried a woman who is now also dead, it's Rachelle, the wife with whom he shared his youth, the one I've known since I was a teenager, who remains the sister-in-law of my heart. After we speak of my mother for a while she offers to notify her children—my niece and two nephews who are scattered around the country. My niece calls back a few hours later to say she's sorry but she can't come to the funeral. I don't hear from either of my nephews, not even the one who was her favorite grandchild.

There's no one else to call. Ninety-four years old and there's no one else to call. She lived a long time, I tell myself; everyone else is dead. But I know it would have been the same at fifty. My heart twists when I come face-to-face with the impoverishment of her life, and a voice inside me cries, *"No one should die that way."* But in truth, she died as she lived, isolated from others by the bitterness, rage, and paranoia that poisoned her life and relationships.

If I had a more mystical temperament, I'd be inclined to think my mother's death on the day before Christmas was her final triumph, her way of making sure I could never enjoy the holiday again. For Christmas had been a sore point between us for many years.

As a child in a Jewish family where we didn't acknowledge the holiday, I always felt excluded and isolated during this season. No celebration of Hanukkah, which in those days wasn't greeted with the kind of fanfare many Jewish families accord it today, could compensate for being left out of Christmas.

Once, when I was about nine years old, I talked Lenny into joining me in saving our pennies so we could buy my mother a Christmas present. I thought about it for weeks, examining all the possibilities, turning them over in my mind again and again, wanting desperately to buy something that would please her, that would bring a loving smile to her lips. Finally, I settled on a pair of silk stockings, a treasured luxury she would never have afforded herself.

On Christmas morning I awoke before dawn and waited impatiently for my mother to arise. Even now, more than sixty years later, I can almost feel again the giddy excitement as I anticipated her pleasure and imagined myself basking in her approval. It seemed like forever before she finally opened her eyes. When she did, my brother and I hopped on the bed, and I handed her our treasure. "Merry Christmas," I cried expectantly. She sat frozen for a moment looking at the small, clumsily wrapped package I pressed upon her as if she couldn't believe her eyes. Then without a word, she raised her hand and slapped me across the face with a blow so hard it sent me tumbling from the bed. The gift, never opened, wound up in the garbage.

I understand now that I had crossed a forbidden border, that giving her a Christmas present was tantamount to announcing that I had joined the *goyim* (Gentiles). Most immigrant parents are ambivalent, both wanting their children to become Americanized and fearing that they'll lose touch with their heritage. For Jews— people who are part of a tribe that has held on to the faith through more than five thousand years of prejudice, discrimination, forced conversions, expulsions, and attempts to exterminate them—the dilemma is compounded by the knowledge that they live in a dominantly Christian country whose seductions offer powerful temptations to their children. And Christmas is the most tantalizing of all, since this is the moment when Jewish children are most likely to suffer their difference most keenly, when their Judaism can feel most burdensome.

But I didn't think any of these things then. Nor, in her characteristic fashion, did my mother make any attempt to explain why she was so angry. The slap and the icy silence I was treated to for the next week or so—a punishment that was much worse than getting hit—were all the explanation I would ever get. For me, however, it was one of the several critical moments of my childhood, moments when I saw my mother through hate-filled eyes and promised myself that I would never be like her—a promise that was never far from my consciousness, even when I couldn't keep it. Or maybe especially when I couldn't keep it.

I swore to myself that no child of mine would have to feel so lonely and excluded at Christmas, a pledge I kept by encouraging my daughter to believe in Santa Claus as a small child and by bringing friends together around our table each year on Christmas day. I didn't flaunt our Christmas activities, but I didn't hide them from my mother either, which brought us into conflict around this holiday in my adulthood, just as it had when I was a child. For my mother, I was an infidel and, worse yet, I was "turning my daughter into a *shikseh*," an apostasy against which she raged. I think now it probably was pain that she felt as well as anger. But my mother could never acknowledge pain, which made it much easier to keep doing what I wanted to do.

Normally, Jewish funerals are held within twenty-four hours after death, but there are certain days in the Jewish calendar when burials are not permitted. This year Christmas Eve is also the first night of Hanukkah, and Jewish law forbids immediate interment. Consequently, my mother will not be buried until Wednesday morning.

We cancel Christmas dinner, of course, and I refuse friends' offers to bring food and comfort. I'm moved by their warmth and caring, but I don't feel much like seeing anyone else right now. So we sit in the living room—Hank, Marci, and I—sometimes silent, sometimes talking quietly about my mother, each of us sharing some part of our experience of her.

Hank remembers his first meeting with her—her cool appraisal, her wariness when he bent to kiss her cheek, her flirtatiousness when he continued his warm and courteous attentions. In the years ahead, he, who loves flowers and fills our home with gorgeous arrangements, would bring her flowers whenever we visited, the first she'd ever received. But while she often said she thought he was "too good" for me, he never got past his outsider status. For my mother, as for so many immigrants trying to make their way in an alien and often hostile culture, if you weren't related by blood, you were outside the magic circle.

Not that being inside the circle was any assurance of acceptance. It was as if she felt that the relationship of blood was so privileged, so permanently fixed, that she had permission to do or say anything she pleased. Marci remembers the pain she felt when, during a visit to my mother when she was twelve years old, she was forced to listen to a tirade of invective about what a "rotten daughter" I was.

"What about good memories?" I ask.

"It's funny, I have lots of them about Grandma Fanny (her birth father's mother) but not about your mother. I never could get close to her. I remember when I came to visit you when you were teaching in New York and Grandma was there. I kept trying to talk to her and tease her to make her laugh. But it was no use. I guess she loved me in her way; I mean she'd say she did, but it never really felt like it."

The time passes slowly. It's three days yet until the funeral; it seems too far away. I understand now why Jews bury their dead so quickly; why they save the ritual mourning period until after the funeral rather than before. It's hard to go on with life while the dead are still around.

I need to mark this moment, but we have no rituals with which to do so. I say the words; Marci reminds me that we can make one, pointing out also that it's the first night of Hanukkah. It's a holiday that has never claimed much of our attention, but now making potato *latkes* (pancakes), the ritual food of this festival, seems the perfect thing to do.

Marci suggests that we go to her house, since we've now been sitting in ours getting progressively more depressed for several hours. I resist at first, feeling somehow that I shouldn't be doing anything that might be remotely pleasurable. But it seems important to her, as if this is the one way she can take care of me. So I agree, and we gather ourselves together for the drive across the bridge to Oakland, where she lives.

By the time we get there Larry is waiting, and he and Hank go to the market while Marci and I set the table and she gets out the menorah she reclaimed from us years ago. It hadn't seen light in our house since she was a child, and she wanted it partly as a reminder of that time in her life and partly because she wanted to light it in her own home—her homage to her Jewishness when she was raising a stepson who himself wasn't Jewish. A few hours later, the menorah lit, we sit down to a traditional Hanukkah *latke* dinner. But first we lift our glasses in a farewell toast to my mother.

We celebrate Hanukkah now, the same dinner at Marci's house each year, although it has grown larger and more inclusive, as friends are invited to share the Festival of Lights with us. My mother, I imagine, would exult in this aftermath of her death, just as it probably would give her pleasure to know that the timing of her death will forever cast a shadow on Christmas for me.

Chapter Four

What is it they say about being careful what you wish for? When my mother was alive and I felt burdened by her care, I kept wondering when it would be my time to be old. Suddenly, "my time" has arrived. It's a strange feeling to stand at the head of the generational queue, to know that I'm *it,* the older generation, no one to stand between me and death. Yet it's not death that troubles me. I have a long acquaintance with thoughts of death, since for a good part of my life suicidal thoughts were my frequent companions.

I don't mean that I'm wholly at ease with confronting the great unknown, the black void that awaits all of us at the end of life. Rather my suicidal reveries were a way to recapture some control in a life that often seemed uncontrollable. As a child, when conflict with my mother became so intense as to seem unbearable, my thoughts about how I could kill myself were both vengeful (I'll show her!) and soothing (I can get away from her any time I really want to!). As a young adult, when periodic bouts of depression left me wondering about the meaning of my life, I thought about ending the meaninglessness.

I'm reasonably certain that I never really meant to kill myself. Thirty years of clinical work, coupled with a lifetime of personal experience, has taught me to respect the paradox that frequently lies at the root of suicidal fantasies: The belief that a person can bring about her own death is often what allows her to keep on living. For me, if I could believe I could opt out when things got too tough, I could define "too tough" as the next level of pain or sorrow, the one that would be worse than anything I was feeling in the moment, and keep on living.

I no longer think about killing myself, but the ease with which my thoughts still turn to death, the deeply felt sense at times that it's easier to die than to live, remains fixed in my internal life. I wonder about this from time to time, especially when I note my husband's firm connection to life and compare it with my own much looser one. Unless he were infirm, he would never say dying is preferable to living; never think, as I sometimes do, that it wouldn't be terrible to die right now.

This isn't depression speaking now, although, as I've said, I've known that in the past. Nor is it that I'm not passionately attached to life while I'm living it. I have always lived with an intensity that makes some people around me tired. It's simply to say that, as I go about trying to find my way into this new stage of my life, it's not dying that engages me. It's the fear that the fires that have fueled my life will soon be banked. *Who will I be then?*

I recall the time long ago when a man I was seeing offered me a marriage that, he promised, would bring with it a life of contentment. *Contentment!* He might as well have proposed death. A great part of me still feels that way, and a voice inside shouts: "I don't want to be content, I want to live." But whether I like it or not, my internal sense of self has been changing for a while, and my mother's death has hastened those changes along.

Having lived in the role of my mother's daughter for over seventy years, it shouldn't surprise me to find that it will take a while to know what to do with that part of me now that it's no longer relevant. But when I awaken in the morning thinking, "Oh God, I haven't called her for a week," it does. Then, when I remember that she's dead, I feel relieved that I can claim my life without the guilt and anger that marked our relationship. But relief and sadness go hand in hand because when she died, something in me died as well. I'll never again be somebody's daughter; that part of my life is over. The roles that defined my relationship with my mother are gone; angers that were so much a part of my inner life have vanished; identities that were mine exist no longer. So it's not just my mother I mourn but yesterday's self. That's part of what grieving is about, the loss of roles that have defined part of the self for so long.

It's true that life is filled with losses as we leave behind one chapter and move into the next. But in those earlier transitions the loss usually is offset by a gain. We leave childhood but gain the freedom and privileges of adulthood; we lose some of that freedom when we become parents but add an important new dimension to our lives; the departure of the children from the nest is a loss that, at the same time, opens new horizons and possibilities for living that were unavailable earlier. Only in death is there nothing but loss, which is, perhaps, why it's so hard for us to confront it.

But I wanted my mother to die. I knew her death wouldn't be an emotional walk in the park for me; there was too much tied up in our relationship for that. But I also looked forward to the peace that the end of this troubled relationship would bring. As with so much in life, however, the anticipation doesn't match the reality. I didn't foresee what it would mean to lose this formidable antagonist of my life. It's as if the force of energy that characterized my personality and charged my life has been dimmed.

After a quarter of a century and nine published books—years during which I forged my identity as a writer and came to feel that putting words on paper was a crucial element of my well-being— I suddenly find myself unable to write. I have a book waiting for its last chapter and a contract for another. But right now I feel empty and have nothing to say. Has my lifetime of work and accomplishment been largely in the service of opposing her? It seems more than a small irony that I, the daughter of an illiterate woman—a woman whose deepest shame was that she never learned to read or write—have made my mark in the world with the written word.

I'm restless, tired of these thoughts, so I leave and go for a favorite walk, down to the bay where I can sit on the seawall and listen to the whisper of the water as it laps the shore. It's a cold, foggy day, but as always there are swimmers in the bay, hardy folk who take on the challenge of these freezing waters throughout the year. I watch the fog's changing patterns as the wind drives it over the Golden Gate Bridge and across the bay. The usual sailboats aren't out in this weather, but two cargo ships, both riding low in the water, pass under the bridge—one coming in, the other going out—and sound their foghorns in greeting. I'm captivated by the sound of foghorns and, since sleep doesn't always come easily to me, I spend many nights listening to their plaintive wail and thinking that this surely must be the loneliest sound on earth.

I love to watch these ships coming and going, and I often spin out romantic fantasies about what they're bringing and what they're taking away. I imagine the time long ago when the early European explorers discovered the trade routes that brought the Western world its first taste of tea and the feel of silk. These extraordinary adventurers have always captured my imagination, and I try to envision the sights that greeted the first explorers who came to this shore. The hills of San Francisco must have been pristine then, no trace of the development that has transformed this place into a vibrant city. What was it like then to sail through the channel now spanned by the Golden Gate Bridge and come upon this wondrous scene, a natural harbor surrounded by a formidable terrain of hills that reach up toward the sky?

As I sit there bundled up against the chill wind and watch the comings and goings of the ships, my mind wanders to other kinds of explorers, the immigrants who have been coming to this country for more than two hundred years, to my parents and their journey from Russia to the United States. It was 1923, less than a year before the United States Congress passed legislation that closed the gates to immigrants from Eastern and Southern Europe for most of the next half century. Since I learned about those immigration laws in high school, I've often thought about the twist of fate that sent my parents on their way just in time for me to grow up as an American rather than a Russian. As a young teenager I would try to picture myself as a Russian girl, try to imagine what I would be doing, who my friends would be, what my life would be like.

I'm reminded of my first visit to the magnificent museum of immigration on Ellis Island and recall the sense I had of walking in my parents' shoes. The pile of battered trunks, suitcases, and baskets that greeted me as I entered the building, the photographs of the immigrants shuffling their way through the entry process, the Great Hall where they gathered to await their fate—all these brought my parents' journey alive.

In my mind's eye I could see them: my father, slender, medium height, neither handsome nor ugly, an ordinary-looking man whose calm gray eyes were his most memorable feature; my mother, not fat but thick, a short woman with a big-breasted peasant's body topped by a head of thick black hair and a face whose youthful prettiness was already fading They were young, twenty-three and twenty-two, but their step was tired as they stood for the first time on American soil holding my seven-month-old brother in their arms, shepherding my father's younger brother who had made the journey with them, and carrying everything they owned in two cardboard suitcases and a straw basket.

The crossing in steerage had been hard—endless days and nights of being jammed together with hundreds of other families, violently rolling winter seas, and the misery of seasickness. The feel of solid ground under their feet was good. But they were anxious as they entered the Great Hall to wait their turn. What if something goes wrong? What if they won't let us in?

It wasn't an idle concern or ordinary immigrant paranoia. My father already had suffered such a setback when, seven years earlier, in the waning months of 1916, he arrived at this very spot with his parents and nine siblings. During the medical examination to which all immigrants were subjected then, the doctor found scabies in the head of five-year-old Benjamin, the youngest child. The rest of the family passed, but the afflicted child was refused admission and scheduled to be returned to the land from which he had just come.

It's not hard to imagine the panic that swept over my grandparents when they heard the news. How could they turn back? A family life disassembled isn't readily put back together again. Everything they owned had been sold to secure the money for passage. There was nothing to return to. And even if they could figure out a way, it meant the end of the dream.

It had taken years of hard work, of scrimping and saving, of planning and scheming, to put together the money for the transatlantic journey. They would never be able to do it again. There were nine other children whose future was at stake. Was it fair to take them back to the threat of pogroms and the life of blocked opportunities that awaited them in the small town outside of Kiev from which they'd come?

Tormented, they made a decision. One of the older children would take Benjamin back until the running sores were fully healed. It wouldn't be long, a few months and they'd be able to rejoin the family. I don't know whether my father, then sixteen years old, volunteered or was tapped for the job. Either way, he got it.

No one knew, of course, that by October 1917 the Communist revolution would have overthrown the Russian czar and the country would be engulfed in a civil war between the forces of the new Communist government and the supporters of the old regime. Nor that in an effort to isolate the revolutionaries and force the Communists from power, the Western nations would ring the newly formed Union of Soviet Socialist Republics with troops that allowed neither entry nor exit.

It took seven more years before my father and uncle could find their way out. Seven years of hiding out from both the Reds and the Whites as the country was engulfed in a civil war; seven years of running to avoid being conscripted into one of the armies; seven years of struggling to support himself and his little brother.

It was toward the end of those years that he met my mother, introduced to her by her older brother for whom he was then working in the underground ghetto economy of Kiev. It's hard to know why they came together; they didn't seem like a very good match. He was a gentle man; she, even by her own account, an angry, impatient woman. Perhaps it was sheer loneliness that united them, perhaps a shared desire for another life, perhaps just the chance of time and place. Certainly she was the driving force in the union, probably the one whose determination finally got them out of the Soviet Union.

My brother, a year and a half older than I, arrived on the scene about a year after they married. By that time my father was once again on the run from the Red Army which was sweeping up every young male in sight. With the financial help of her older brother, my mother, father, uncle, and infant brother stole out of Kiev hidden in the back of a horse-drawn lorry. It took them weeks to make their way across the border, then to Bremen in Germany, where they secured passage on the ship that brought them to this country.

I was born in 1924, just ten months after they arrived in Philadelphia, where most of my father's family had settled. They were a large, unruly, and boisterous brood, that family. Ordinary conversation was carried on at ear-splitting decibels. I don't know which was worse: the men's booming voices or the women's shrill ones. But together they created a roar that no child's voice could penetrate. By the time I was three years old, I would sit at family gatherings with my hands over my ears in a vain attempt to shut out the noise. We kids also learned quickly that when there was a dispute or an argument—which happened often—it was best to get out of the way. Not that they were physically violent. But the verbal fisticuffs were equally frightening to a small child.

When I think about it now, I assume this noisy, disputatious style was partly cultural. Jews have a long history of debate and argument, a legacy that's deeply embedded in Jewish lore and whose record is written in the Talmud, the Jewish holy book. There, the rabbis of old chronicled their heated disputes about the meaning of *the word,* each demanding to be heard, each arguing in painstaking detail for his point of view, each insisting that his interpretation was the right one. A tradition that continues into the present as the rabbis revisit the old debates and offer their own meticulous explications of the text.

Whatever part the culture played in forming the ethos of my father's family, the kind of tumult I remember undoubtedly was also a product of its size. With ten children, their mates, and their offspring, if you wanted to be heard, to claim your space, you probably had to shout.

My mother rarely talked about her own family, all of whom were left behind in Russia. Nor did she ever see or hear from them again. When I was older, I would plead with her to tell me who they were, what they did, where they lived. But most of the time she met my questions with an impatient "There's nothing to tell. They're dead." Then she'd repeat what I'd heard a thousand times: "The day I got on the ship I swore I'd never speak another word of Russian in my life." It wasn't just the language she rejected, it was the whole life she had lived until that time.

I know now that this was the only way she could cope with the pain of leaving all that was familiar. It's not an uncommon psychological defense in the face of such loss; I see it often in my clinical practice. If you shut out the past, build a wall between yesterday and today, between yourself and your memories, it eases the pain of separation. But it's costly, since it's not possible to seal off the past so profoundly and still remain open to the present.

What I know about my mother's life in Russia is gleaned from the little bits and pieces she grudgingly told me when, I suppose, it was easier to answer my questions than to fend me off. She was the youngest of four children—two brothers who were substantially older and a sister who was closer to her own age. When she was twelve years old, her mother died, and shortly thereafter her father remarried a woman who became her wicked stepmother. By then her brothers were living in homes of their own; only my mother and her sister were left to live in the newly constituted household.

Her sister got along with her stepmother; my mother did not. After about a year, therefore, she was sent to live in a neighboring town with one of her older brothers. There, according to her story, she became the Cinderella of the family, relegated to the most menial household chores and a cot in the cellar.

However her stories may have been colored by time and bitterness, one thing is clear: From the time her mother died, she experienced herself as an outsider in her family, an unwelcome intruder who eventually was sent away. A scenario that was replayed when she came to this country and found herself in the middle of my father's family. For while they were a quarrelsome and rivalrous bunch who descended into ugly enmities among themselves, they shared that peculiar trait, so common in families, of banding together against anyone who was not one of them. And in-laws definitely were out.

For my mother, it was a setup for disaster. She was a bitter, angry, distrustful woman who was always ready for battle even when no one wanted to fight. In my father's family, where fighting was as normal as breathing, she had found her match and was quickly embroiled in conflict with various aunts and uncles as well as with my grandmother, a tough matriarch with whom no one trifled.

My mother's tirades against one or another of her in-laws form some of my earliest and most uncomfortable memories. For it didn't take much for her rage at them to spill over on to whomever happened to be in her path, which all too often was her husband and children.

My father got it because he was one of "them"—"a Breslow" she would say, spitting out our surname as if it were an epithet. With me, it was less clear, more as if my presence itself enraged her than because of anything I did or said. Years later, when I understood something about family dynamics and the cost to a child of a parent's premature death, I wondered whether the particular hostility she directed at me was born of the need to mother a daughter when she herself had not had a mother. Only with my brother, not only her favored child but the one who was defined as delicate because of a mysterious childhood malady, did she make some effort to contain her rages. Although even with him she often wasn't successful.

During those early years of my life, we lived as most new immigrant families did. Poor, depressed, exploited by landlords who rented substandard dwellings at above-standard rents, by employers who knew they could hire desperate men like my father for less than they had to pay American workers, by the budding immigrant entrepreneurs who cheated the newcomers in a variety of ways. After trying his hand unsuccessfully at several trades, my father became a furrier and, with help from my grandparents, rented a shop from which he would ply his trade.

We lived behind the store, on a street lined with other small shops, family enterprises in which parents and any children old enough to make change toiled daily except Saturday, the Jewish Sabbath, and Sunday, when all of Philadelphia was shut down by the blue laws that held that any commerce on Sunday was a violation of the day to be given over to the Christian God.

My father's store was bare except for two big tables at each end of the room on which he stretched the fur he hoped to make into coats for women who could afford them. But his customers were few. We entered our apartment, a flat in which all the rooms were off a long center hall, from a door at the back of shop. My most vivid memory is of the hallway, which was so dark I was afraid to be there alone, and the kitchen, in which stood a small square table covered with a flowered oil cloth surrounded by four rickety chairs, one of them with its top sheared off. The large round scar I carry on my right thigh from when I slipped from the table (I have no idea why I was on it) and impaled myself on that chair has fixed it forever in my memory.

I have only spotty early memories of my father, but one of my fondest is located in this store. I'm about three years old, and I'm running into the store with my mother in pursuit. I don't know what I did to make her so angry, but I can still feel the urgency to get out of her way. Like a little whirlwind, I fly past my father, scramble under the stretching table at which he's working, and cover my ears to shut out her angry voice. I'm not sure what happened after that, what they said to each other, what he did, but in fantasy, at least, I see him standing in front of the table, his legs and arms akimbo, his soft voice placating her and protecting me.

Was my father the good guy in the family? Or is this just the imaginative reconstruction of a small child who was, even then, in combat with her mother and needed to believe there was someone around who could offer protection? I don't know. I remember him largely as a phantom presence in the house, kind but withdrawn, as if all he wanted was to stay out of my mother's way. But that, too, may be a projection of my own wishes at the time. I'll never know because he died when I was five years old.

Chapter Five

It was the middle of the night when I heard a crash in the hallway that awakened me out of a sound sleep. Frightened, I climbed out of bed and ran into the hall to see my mother on her knees beside my father who was lying on the floor looking deathly white.

I don't remember much more about that night, only that someone put me back to bed, where I lay shivering and listening to the commotion outside the bedroom door. The next morning an aunt was there to give us breakfast. My mother, she said, would be back soon. But what may have been soon to an adult felt like an eternity to a frightened five-year-old.

I can still recall the cold fear that clutched my heart that morning. And the questions: Where could they have gone? They'd always before been there when I woke up. Why was my aunt here instead of taking care of her own children? What happened to my father? The last I saw him he was lying on the floor, white and motionless.

My brother was at the table, his shoulders hunched, thick glasses sliding down his nose as he peered about anxiously. In our characteristic ways, he sat quietly spooning his cereal into his mouth while I, refusing to eat, jumped up and ran toward my parents' bedroom with my aunt in pursuit. She caught me and tried to hold me still, telling me again that my mother would be back soon. But I was too frightened to be contained. I wriggled out of her arms and continued my flight down the hall until I was safely under my parents' bed. It seemed to my five-year-old mind that I was there for a long time before an older cousin, whom I loved, came and coaxed me out. As we walked down the hall, the door that separated the apartment from the store opened and I saw my mother, nearly prostrate with grief, being carried into the house by one of my uncles.

My brother and I ran to her, but my uncle fended us off while he led her to a chair in the living room. She sat there, quietly at first, her body rigid, her face contorted into a mask of a pain, seeming not even to notice her children tugging at her. Then the keening began, a terrible heart-stopping, high-pitched wail that tore at my soul and sent me back down the hall and under the bed.

Although no one had telephones then, the news spread quickly, brought, I assume, by a family courier who was dispatched through the Philadelphia neighborhood we all lived in. Soon our small apartment overflowed with family members— aunts, uncles, cousins, my grandparents—some of them spilling out of the living room and lining the hallway. From my place under the bed I could hear the rise and fall of their voices, the sniffling that told me people were crying, my mother's lament. I lay there trembling, hugging myself and wishing for the comfort of someone else's arms but afraid of what I'd see if I came out of hiding. I must have slept, because the next thing I remember an uncle was pulling me out from under the bed and carrying me into the room where my mother sat just as I had left her.

The rest of the day is a jumble of blurred images: Lenny and I sitting huddled in a corner while the talk swirled around us; asking where my father was and getting a pat on the head for an answer; my mother weeping and conjuring with God. Nobody talked to us about what happened; no one said the word *dead*.

It wasn't until I was taken to the interment at the cemetery the next day that I knew my father had died, although I'm sure I had no idea yet what that meant. My memory of the funeral is hazy and fragmented: the ache in my arm as it stretched up for what seemed like forever so that an aunt could hold on to my hand; my view of black-clad legs, the only thing I could see unless I looked straight up at the sky; my brother, skinny, pale, looking as frightened as I felt.

In my mind's eye I can still see the five-year-old I was then—a little girl standing silent and solemn, eyes wide with . . . what? Anxiety? Dread? Did my skin feel prickly because of the hot sun beating down on me? Or was it fear that rippled across my bare arms and down my back and made me want to run?

I can almost smell again the sweat as people seemed to melt down in the soggy heat. I was too little to see what was happening, but I could hear the muffled voice of the rabbi and the snuffling and sniffling as people wept. Then, the same ear-piercing shriek I'd heard the day before shattered the stillness and echoed through the cemetery. I couldn't see her, but I knew it was my mother's voice. Terrified, I wrenched my hand away from my aunt, covered my ears, and tried to run. Anywhere, just to get away from the sound. But someone caught and held me until I collapsed weeping in his arms. No matter how many years passed I never went to my father's grave again without hearing that anguished keening, even when my mother wasn't with me.

I know now that on the night of his collapse my father was taken to the hospital by ambulance and died several hours later of an internal hemorrhage brought about by unattended bleeding ulcers. As I grew older and thought about the amount of neglect necessary for an otherwise healthy twenty-nine-year-old man to die of such ulcer complications, I decided that his death was a form of suicide, the only way he could get out of living with my mother. Many years later, when I told this to a physician friend, he smiled and said, "Maybe so, but you should know that in those days we didn't have the treatment we have now, and death from bleeding ulcers wasn't so uncommon."

I also know that poor people, now as well as then, often don't go to doctors when they should because they can't afford either the time or money. But then, and for a long time afterward, I needed to believe that my father allowed himself to die to escape my mother. It made sense not only of his death but of my confusing and contradictory feelings about it. Sometimes I'd hug those thoughts to myself, feeling comforted by them because they justified my embattled relationship with my mother. If he, a grown man, couldn't live with her peacefully, how could I be expected to do so? At other moments I'd be furious with him for leaving me to deal with her unprotected for the rest of my life—a legacy that, years later, infused my relationships with men with an unwholesome brew of a longing for constancy and a mistrustful watchfulness that was my defense against another abandonment.

Chapter Six

It's three weeks since my mother died, and I'm at the airport awaiting a flight that will take me to Boston where I'll keynote a conference on balancing family and work in this modern age. I've been interested in this topic since my daughter was a little girl and I was caught in the conflict between the dictates of the culture about what a good mother was supposed to do and my own needs for some stimulation outside the home. As I moved in and out of the labor force during those early years of my child's life, neither home nor office felt fully comfortable. When I went to work, I was anxious and guilty about not being at home with my daughter; when I quit and became a stay-at-home mom, I was restless and bored.

It's not an accident that these issues, which have been a problem for women for a very long time, were largely neglected until very recently. Women, especially poor women, have always worked—in the fields and the factories, in the boardinghouses where they cared for the single men who lived there, in their own homes where they did a variety of tasks from sewing for the rich to washing their dirty clothes. But the problems seem more urgent now, less manageable, partly at least because it's no longer just poor women who leave their children every day for work outside the home.

Well over 60 percent of all women with children under three and 80 percent with children between six and seventeen are now in the labor force. And when it's middle- and upper-middle-class families who face the issues and conflicts that confront two working parents, everyone—from governmental agencies to the private foundations who fund conferences like the one I'll be speaking at tomorrow—pays attention.

Right now I'm struck by the irony that at the very moment I'm flying off to talk about the collision between the demands of work and family, I'm caught once again in my own personal conflict between the two. A few days ago Marci found a lump in her breast and a biopsy is scheduled for tomorrow. It has been an anxious time for all of us, and my first impulse was to cancel this trip so that I could be with her through this—the waiting and the surgery. She, of course, insists that I go to Boston and assures me she'll be fine. "Larry and Daddy will be right here, and you'll come back on Saturday, so please go and don't worry."

Don't worry! How does a mother not worry when her daughter faces the threat of breast cancer?

I have endless "should I/shouldn't I" conversations with myself. "The lecture was scheduled a year ago; I can't bow out now. But Marci may have breast cancer; doesn't that count? Yes, but my being here won't change that. No, but how will I feel if I hear that news when I'm three thousand miles away? Worse yet, how will she feel when I'm not here to help her through that moment?"

I talk with Hank, who thinks I should go. "It isn't just for her," I tell him. "I need to be here for me."

"I know it will be hard not being here, but you have this commitment and you should probably fulfill it. Marci will most likely be fine, and I'll call you the minute we get word of the results. By that time your lecture will be over and you can take the next plane home if the news is bad."

"Damnit, there's never a time in a mother's life when she's not juggling the competing demands of work and family, is there?"

"I don't know," he replies, "this one would engage a father's attention, too."

"Yeah, but he'd know he had to take care of business and that Mom would be on the job with the kid."

"Well," he says, "I guess you have a choice now. You can let me be on the kid job while you take care of business, or you can insist that Mom is the only one who can do it right. Seems to me," he adds with a teasing glint in his eye, "you've written about women who do that, then complain about how they can't count on their men."

"I was talking about doing the laundry, not about leaving a child who might have a deadly disease," I reply irritably. But I know he's right; most probably the lump will turn out to be benign and if not (I can hardly think the thought) I can be home in a few hours.

Now, sitting in the airport, I try to distract myself from my worries about Marci and pull out my lecture notes to review them. But my mind slides from the work to my mother, as it has surprisingly often in these weeks. As I contemplated her death, waited for it, wished for it, I assumed that my dominant feeling would be relief. Instead, I find myself doing something like mourning. I don't mean that I miss my mother's presence, at least not the mother I had. But in the middle of a busy day I suddenly find thoughts of her floating around in my head, and I descend into sadness.

The image of her as I said my last good-bye is engraved in my brain—her eyes closed, her sparse gray hair lank against the pillow, her wrinkled face seeming to have collapsed in on itself, her hands clenched into fists that tug at my heart. *Right down to the last she was ready to fight.* Now, as I relive that scene yet again, I feel a deep sorrow that, even as she prepared to die, she couldn't unclench her fists.

As always, however, my thoughts about my mother are never wholly unambivalent, and I can't help comparing how she behaved when I was ill and in need with my response now to my daughter's plight. Like the time I gave birth to my first child. After a brutal seventy-two hours of labor, my daughter died a few hours later. When my mother heard the news she rushed to my hospital room and strode in holding her head and shrieking, "*Gottenyu,* how could you do this to me?" I don't know just how long it was, perhaps five minutes or so, before she stopped weeping and railing at God for his cruelty to her and made some effort to attend to how I was feeling.

I'm not suggesting that she didn't care about what happened to me; when a child is suffering a mother feels the pain as if it were her own. And that was precisely the problem. She couldn't separate her pain from mine, couldn't see my anguish because she was so overwhelmed with her own. When I think about what my daughter might suffer, I know how my mother felt. And the ache in my heart when I try to touch the idea that Marci could die is nearly unbearable. But I haven't left her out of the equation. It's her anguish, her fear, the threat to her body, her life that are uppermost in my mind right now. My anxieties can wait.

The announcement that my flight is ready for boarding rouses me from my musings. By the time I collect my things and get to the gate, a long line has already formed. I move into place and follow the crowd as we shuffle forward slowly. Finally in my seat, I return to my work, thinking about some ideas from my most recent research that I want to incorporate into my lecture.

I have been interviewing men and women between the ages of forty and sixty-five, some who married young and had children soon after, others who delayed family building until much later. It's an interesting study because, unlike earlier generations when adult lives generally moved along a narrow timetable, now some fifty-year-old couples have grown children while others are chasing after toddlers. Which means their interests, needs, lifestyles, and plans for the future are wholly at odds.

Two hours later I look up startled at how quickly the time has gone. I get up to stretch and walk up and down the aisle, irritating the flight attendants as I inch my way past their carts. But I have no choice. Since my first pregnancy more than fifty years ago, I have been vulnerable to deep vein blood clots in my legs—a danger that's heightened by the cramped conditions of modern air travel. So I spend a good part of every flight on my feet as I try to keep the blood circulating freely.

Back in my seat, I put my work away and dig a novel out of the all-purpose tote bag that goes with me everywhere I travel. Moments later I feel a pain in my back so sharp that it doubles me up and leaves me gasping for breath. I know at once that this is what I've expected for years, a pulmonary embolus, a blood clot that formed in my leg and, pushed along by the rush of blood in my veins, has traveled to my lungs. I have been warned often by my doctors about the danger of this condition, so I know I might die right now. But in the moment it's not fear I feel but disbelief at the irony of the timing. *Oh no, damnit, not now; I can't die now when I finally have a chance to live in this world without her.*

I break out in a sweat as I grapple with the pain and grope in my tote for the ibuprofen and aspirin I always carry with me. It's not just the pain I'm trying to contain but the clotting itself, for I know from long experience that these can offer a moderately effective treatment when the standard blood-thinning drugs aren't immediately available. I swallow two ibuprofen and four aspirin tablets and push my seat back, trying not to panic.

The man in the seat next to me has been asleep for most of the flight, but now he stirs, awakened by my fitful squirming as I try to find some comfortable position. He glances over and straightens in his seat. "You look like death warmed over," he says. "Are you all right?"

If it didn't hurt so much to breathe I'd laugh at his choice of words. "If he only knew," I think. Aloud I say with an attempt at a smile, "Thanks for the compliment."

He wants to call a flight attendant, but I stop him. The only thing they can do is put the plane down in some godforsaken place in the middle of the country, and the idea of being hospitalized so far from home upsets me more than the pain. I assure him that I'll be all right and somehow, despite what I know, I believe it. He reminds me to call for help if I need it, then pulls out a laptop computer and settles down to his own work. Right now all I want to do is lie back, wait for the pain to abate, and continue to dose myself with ibuprofen and aspirin.

In my head I know I'm risking my life, but I seem unable to do anything else. So I lie there thinking that this wouldn't be a bad way to die. I've always said I want to go out at my peak, that I didn't want to drag my body or mind to the kind of miserable end my mother suffered, where all that was left was a shell of the person she had been.

I've watched great athletes continue to play well beyond when they should have retired. I can imagine how hard it must be to give up the adulation of the crowds, the glory of another touchdown pass, another home run, another victory at the finish line. But when I see their waning powers displayed before the world, I feel saddened for them. No, more than saddened, shamed—a visceral response to their humiliation that's undoubtedly a reflection of my own fears about myself.

Now, thirty thousand feet in the air, I worry about leaving my daughter and my husband so suddenly, knowing that the news of my death will be devastating to them. But for me, I can think of a lot worse ways to go than in the middle of living my life fully. Then I remember Marci and the lump in her breast, and I descend into panic: *No, I can't die now; she needs me.*

By the time the plane touches down in Boston, the pain has diminished enough so that I can breathe, if only shallowly. I know I should go to the hospital at once, but my fear of being hospitalized three thousand miles from everyone I love overcomes common sense. Even under ideal circumstances, hospitals make me anxious, a remnant, I think, of the time when my brother and I had our tonsils removed.

He was six, I was four and a half and, unlike these days, parents then weren't permitted to stay in the hospital with their children. Sometime in the middle of the night after the surgery I awoke to hear my brother, who was sleeping in the next bed, sounding as if he were choking. I climbed out of bed and found him lying in a pool of blood. Unable to shout for help because my postsurgical throat allowed for only a bare whisper, I flew out of the room and through the hospital hallway until I literally ran into a nurse who, registering my distress at once, picked me up and ran with me back to the ward.

The next morning, as word spread through the ward that I'd saved my brother's life, I became the heroine of the day, and nurses and doctors came to visit and tell me how brave I had been. Even my mother, from whom I had already learned to expect reproach more readily than approval, lavished me with loving praise. I basked in the unaccustomed attention from the adult world, but it's the memory of the loving eyes with which my mother looked at me that day that can still stir me to tears of joy.

Where was that memory when I needed it, I wonder as I lean back in the taxi that's taking me to my hotel. Where was it when, on the day she died, I searched my mind and heart in vain for some sign of her love? A voice inside reminds me that, despite all my efforts to the contrary, I am my mother's daughter, that I, too, can ward off pain with anger, that to recall the good times in the moment of her death was to open the floodgates of a lifetime of pain I wasn't yet prepared to handle.

I'm caught now between pleasure in having found the memory and pain in the realization of how few such moments were. But whatever my feelings at this time, the lasting effect of that childhood incident has been to make me uneasy and somewhat fearful about hospitals. I have, of course, overcome that fear in the past and can do it again if I have to. But I can't imagine calling home to tell them I'm in a hospital in Boston when Marci is due for a biopsy tomorrow morning. None of the scenarios I can conjure up are acceptable.

If I'm hospitalized here, it will be a few weeks before any doctor will allow me to fly across the country again. If, on hearing that, Marci decides to delay her surgery so she can be with me, we'll all continue to live in fear about what awaits her. If she has the biopsy and the news is bad, it will be a nightmare for us to be in hospitals on different coasts.

So, although I know it's unwise, I also know that I will not go to a hospital in Boston so long as I can make the choice. Instead, I phone one of my hosts, explain that I was taken ill on the plane, and apologize for missing the dinner with the conference committee that has been planned in my honor. He's gracious and concerned, but I can hear the undercurrent of anxiety in his voice. Since the conference program is built around my opening remarks, he worries about whether I'll be able to give my lecture in the morning. How can I promise? I can only try to assure him that I will be all right after a good night's sleep.

But before I can think about that, I call the airline to find out whether I can get home on a late-morning flight. This time I don't worry about the cost and reserve a first-class seat so that I can lie down for the five-and-a-half-hour flight. That done, I take another ibuprofen and aspirin cocktail and crawl into bed where I lie, curled up in the fetal position, which seems to ease the pain somewhat, and doze fitfully through the night.

At eight-thirty the next morning I'm on the lecture platform. I still can't take a deep breath, but I manage the pain well enough to give my lecture and spend another half hour answering questions. Then a car speeds me to Logan Airport, where I have a few minutes before I have to board my flight.

It's still early in San Francisco, so I rush to a phone in the hope that I can catch Hank before he goes to the hospital to be with Marci. He's just leaving when the phone stops him and I tell him I'm on my way home. Uneasy, he immediately asks what's wrong. I don't want to leave him pacing helplessly over both his daughter and his wife for the next several hours, so I give him my flight number and reassure him with some empty words about wanting to be there when Marci gets home from the hospital. I think he believes me, since he knows how anxious I've been about her. But even if he doesn't, whatever he might imagine can't be as bad as hearing the reality at this distance.

By the time I finish talking with him, my flight is called. As soon as we're airborne, I call my doctor who, fortunately, has just walked into his office and takes the call. His usually calm, unflappable manner deserts him when he hears my story. "I can't believe you got back on a plane," he says helplessly. "Find out if there's a doctor on board and have him take a look at you."

"What can he do now?" I ask.

"He can decide to tell them to land the plane and get you to a hospital."

Since that's exactly what I want to avoid, I demur, and instead find myself reassuring my doctor. "No, I think the worst has passed and I want to come home. Just tell me what to do when I get there."

He sighs, defeated, "Get yourself to the emergency room at CPMC [the hospital where he's affiliated]. I'll call and tell them to call me as soon as you get there."

When I deplane in San Francisco, I catch sight of Hank as I'm coming up the ramp and wave. He responds with a gesture, a raised hand with thumb and forefinger making a circle that says she's okay. For the moment I forget my own pain as I feel a surge of joy that brings tears to my eyes. She's okay; she doesn't have cancer.

I don't have to say much when I come up to face him; he needs only to look at me to know something is terribly wrong. I tell him what I know, and we go at once to the emergency room at the hospital while he fills me in on the results of Marci's biopsy. It was a tumor, not a cyst, but it's benign. Wonderful word *benign*. I want to stop and call her but he refuses, insisting that we get to the hospital at once. "She's tired and sleepy from the anesthetic and you'll only disturb her rest," he argues.

He's right. Besides, what will I say to her? I certainly can't burden her with my news right now. Let her rest; tomorrow is plenty of time to talk to her.

A half hour later we arrive at the emergency room, there to wait . . . and wait . . . and wait. Now that I've arrived home safely and feel the comfort of my husband at my side, the fear I've kept at bay for the last two days turns my stomach into knots and makes it even harder to breathe than it has been. I can feel depression descending on me as I sit in this bleak room huddled in pain.

The waiting room is a small, cheerless place with walls that are badly in need of some fresh paint and chairs that long ago saw better days. I occupy myself with watching the others around me: an anxious mother holding a whimpering child on her lap; a man, limping, supporting himself on the shoulder of another; a woman whose grotesquely swollen face suggests a serious allergic reaction; another, probably the victim of domestic abuse, staring blankly ahead as she holds an arm in a homemade sling close to her chest and her swollen eye blackens as I watch; and four or five others whose complaints aren't so obvious. No one speaks. We don't grumble to each other about the wait, don't wonder aloud what's taking so long, don't talk about the ailments that brought us together here. We're each wrapped in our own private misery.

After three interminable hours it's finally my turn. I'm taken into a cubicle where I tell my story to the attending doctor who stares at me in disbelief. "Are you telling me you flew home from Boston with a pulmonary embolus?" Feeling stupid, I mumble my assent. Suddenly there's a whirlwind of activity as they hook me up to machines, prepare to take X-rays, and try to reach my internist. Hank hovers over me anxiously, but all I can think is "I've been trying to tell someone my story for hours and NOW they're in a panic!"

After a few more hours of frenetic activity and several sets of progressively more complicated X-ray studies, the results are in: I've had a pulmonary embolus and my lungs are functioning at a dramatically reduced capacity. Eight hours after I entered the emergency room, I'm finally admitted to the hospital and taken to a room upstairs, an IV dispensing heparin (a fast-acting blood thinner) into my veins trailing the gurney on which they wheel me away. Everyone agrees that it was madness to continue the flight to Boston, worse yet to fly home the next day. But all agree also that medicating myself with ibuprofen and aspirin probably saved my life.

Me? I'm scared and also relieved. I know it was crazy to risk coming home, but I also know I had to do it, had to come back to this life where I love and am loved, where I could be with my daughter if she needed me, where, whether in life or death, I can see the fruit of my struggle to be different from my mother.

Chapter Seven

I wake with a start, my heart pounding, my body bathed in sweat, and sit up so hurriedly that I dislodge the IV that's dripping the life-saving heparin into my veins. Where am I? I stare blankly at the needle dangling from the tape to which it's still attached and watch the blood oozing from the vein in the back of my hand as if it isn't mine. Yesterday's events come back to me slowly as I recognize my hospital room, but the dream that awakened me holds me in its grip.

I'm in a strange place that looks like a huge densely forested but well-tended garden. Someone has built a series of slate steps to make it easier to navigate the hilly, rock-strewn terrain. Some people are with me, Hank, I think, and some others I can't identify, but I'm not paying attention to them. Instead, I'm watching a white-haired old woman some distance away as she shakily descends a flight of steps. I know she's going to fall and shout to her to be careful, but there's nothing to hold on to. I run toward her and hear Hank's voice behind me calling me back, but I can't stop. It's suddenly urgent that I reach her before she falls.

I'm running as fast as I can, slipping and sliding up and down the hills that separate us, but it feels as if I'm moving in slow motion, as if a huge weight is pushing against my chest and holding me back. As I get closer, I see it's my mother. I try to shout, to tell her to hold on, that I'll be right there, but the words come out in a whisper. Helpless I watch as she loses her footing altogether and tumbles head over heels down the steep flight of stairs. When I finally get to her she's lying in a crumpled heap at the foot of the steps.

The blouse she's wearing apparently tore in the fall; her exposed breasts lie flat against her chest, empty and wrinkled with age. I cringe; I don't want to see what age does, don't want to know that this could be me. I reach down to pull her up, but she stands without any help and begins to brush herself off. I'm startled as I look at her more closely and see I've made a mistake. It's not my mother at all, it's me.

I pull myself back to the present and push the call button for a nurse who comes at once and busies herself with reinserting the IV needle. While she fusses and reminds me that I have to be more careful, I lie back and try to calm myself. But the symbolism of the dream won't let me go. I've spent my life in a love-hate ambivalence with my mother, trying to reach her at the same time that I moved as far away as I could. There were periods, sometimes years, when I actually believed I had left her behind—that I had rooted her out of my inner life, that I had completed my lifetime project of disidentifying with her—only to find her popping back again at some unexpected moment. Now here she was, reminding me again, as she did in those rare moments when I did something that pleased her (most often when she was showing off my report card or when someone remarked that I was a beautiful child) that "the apple doesn't fall far from the tree."

I hated hearing those words when I was a child. They made me want to scream, "I don't want to be like you." I wanted her approval for who I was, not for my looks, over which I had no control, or for my grades in school. I was deeply resentful when she took credit for my accomplishments at school and used them to enhance herself publicly, while privately the line in the house was "Your brother's really the smart one; you just get good grades because you study hard." A claim I believed for many years despite all the evidence to the contrary.

As an adult my mother's response to any of my accomplishments became something of a joke, although one that carried its edge of pain. She sniffed dismissively when I got my doctorate, "You can't give me a prescription, so what kind of doctor are you?" and shrugged indifferently at each new book I published, "Other daughters take their mother to lunch every week; you write books." Sometimes she'd find some use for one of the books

I sent, like propping up the fan in her window. Mostly they just disappeared, lost in her tiny one-room apartment. "How do I know what happened to it?" she'd say when I asked. But she retained bragging rights in public and boasted to neighbors about her "daughter the doctor." Not, mind you, without adding the lament, "Some people are lucky, they have a son a doctor, I have a daughter."

Whether as child or adult, neither her pride in my accomplishments nor her diminishment of them was easy for me. When privately she ignored or dismissed my achievements at school or elsewhere, I felt hurt and angry. When she claimed them in public with words that suggested that she and I were alike, it wasn't any better. In fact, there was nothing she could say that was right, nothing that would soothe the complicated mix of pain and rancor that lived alongside the pleasure in her approval and the fear that, despite all my efforts, I really was like her.

My renunciation notwithstanding, I have long known that I am my mother's daughter. And now, as I deal with her death and my own aging, that knowledge strikes me with an anxiety I thought was long gone. *I don't want to live and die as she did; I won't!*

I know somewhere in the reasonable part of myself that it's highly unlikely that anything about my life, whether living or dying, will ever resemble hers. I know, too, that while I am my mother's daughter, I am not her. Yet, as I lie in my hospital bed reliving the dream, reason deserts me and I can't separate the two. I look at my hands and, like the anorexic who sees fat where others see emaciation, I see age spots and short, stubby fingers not visible to anyone else. I push them under the blanket, out of sight. I can hide my hands but the dream image of my mother turning into me, of that ugly old woman actually being me, seems burned into my brain.

It's a relief when my doctor comes in looking concerned and gives me something else to think about. The blood tests they take every few hours tell him I'm not responding to the medication as quickly as he had hoped; something he calls my *pro time* (the measure of my blood–clotting factor) is much too low. I'll soon learn a lot about pro time counts, since my doctor has told me that I will be on a blood thinner for the rest of my life, which means my pro time will have to be monitored regularly for as long as I live. But right now it's just another of the words I've been hearing since yesterday, words so unfamiliar that they don't yet have any internal resonance.

When the doctor leaves, my mind fixes on these words that have no real meaning to me and sends me back to my childhood when English was still a foreign language. Yiddish was the language of the home I grew up in as well as the tongue of most of the Philadelphia community in which we lived. Neighbors, shopkeepers, the local agencies that helped immigrants resettle all spoke Yiddish or had Yiddish-speaking staff members. Even the older kids who were already in school often lapsed into Yiddish on the street, for that was the language of their private world, the language that carried a special resonance because it was connected to the family, to the place where they belonged as they struggled to find their way in a world that was less than welcoming

School was my first real brush with English but, although I was just one of many non-English-speaking children in my classroom, none of the programs that so commonly ease the way for immigrant children today was available then. The teacher helped us with a word when we got stuck, but she turned a deaf ear when, in frustration, a child broke into a foreign language, whether Yiddish or Italian, the other large group of immigrant children in the schools I attended. The rules were clear: We were to speak only English while they inducted us into American ways with a fervor that suggested we were embarrassing reminders of a past they wanted to leave behind.

They weren't unkind, these teachers. But in a land that invites immigrants, then holds them and their culture in contempt, it's common for the newly Americanized to be anxious about their status, to fear they will be judged and measured by their countrymen who haven't yet learned how to be proper Americans. My teachers, who often were young Jewish women just a generation away from the immigrant experience, were, therefore, exquisitely sensitive to the lapses of their Jewish students and were determined to turn us into reasonable facsimiles of American children as quickly as possible.

For me, learning the language and ways of America was easier than for some others partly because I had so little to hold on to from the past. Whatever safety and comfort existed in my family life was shattered by the death of my father and our move to New York. My anger at my mother, my growing determination not to be like her, found a home in my teachers' attitudes, and I grasped eagerly at their teaching, wanting to emulate them, to be an American, like them, not an immigrant, like my mother. If she embodied the old ways, I would reach for the new. If she spoke Yiddish, I would speak English. If she couldn't read, I would grow to love books. For it was only by becoming an American, the *real* American that my mother would never be, that I could believe I could be different from her.

But giving up the language that greeted me at birth, that framed my world from infancy through early childhood, wasn't quite so simple as I had imagined. I don't just mean that it was hard to learn English. That was true, but far easier than the psychological feat necessary to abandon my mother tongue since, in the shift from Yiddish to English, the world, for a time, lost much of its color and meaning. For a language is more than its words and syntax; it's a way of thinking about the world, of meeting it, of being in it. When we learn a language, we absorb its aura—its rhythms, its color, its emotion, its lightness and darkness, its subtleties of expression and meaning. To give it up means relinquishing a part of ourselves, the part that experienced the world through that language.

True, the new language eventually finds its own place in our internal life and its words their own imagery. But it doesn't happen quickly, even in childhood. It was a long time before the word *tree* carried the associations that gave its Yiddish equivalent, *boim,* its emotional power, before I could associate it with the images of the vibrant, changing, living thing whose leafy branches shaded me on a hot summer day. I understood that they were the same objects, but the word itself had no evocative power. It was a word without pictures, a word sundered from the thing it was meant to represent.

As both the internal and external pressures toward Americanization increased, I became more and more alienated from my past. This is one of the uncounted costs of the prejudice immigrants meet when they come to this land of their dreams. As their children endeavor to be accepted by the world around them, they adopt the public attitudes as their own and try to protect themselves from the barbs and jeers by distancing themselves from their heritage and shrinking from any public expression of their difference.

In my own life this meant that I wanted to forget I was the child of a Russian immigrant who could barely speak English, forget I ate pumpernickel instead of white bread, gefilte fish instead of peanut butter and jelly. All I wanted was to be an ordinary American. Although what that meant in positive terms was something of a mystery. The negative side was perfectly clear: Being American meant giving up all visible signs of being Jewish. A nearly impossible task, since being Jewish was second only to being poor in coloring the experience of my youth. It wasn't something I could put on or take off, something I could leave behind when I wanted to. Being Jewish was who I was, a part of my identity as surely as the shape of my body or the color of my eyes.

I'm saddened now when I recall how I cringed when I heard my mother's accented English in public; when I think about how much I wanted her to come to school during Open School Week so I could show off how smart I was, and how mortified I was when she came and her foreignness stood revealed; when I remember my reluctance to ask an American classmate into my home for fear she'd sneer at what she saw and heard there.

I wish these things hadn't mattered so much. But they mattered precisely because of the unrelenting pressure to become an American, pressure that came not just from the outside world but from the immigrant Jewish community as well—a community of

people who mocked their less socialized and assimilated countrymen as "greenhorns."

I still loathe that word, can still feel the shame and self-hatred
I experienced when I first heard it shouted at me. It was on the
playground, just a few days after I started school. A girl, probably
a little older than I and certainly better able to speak English, said
something I didn't understand. In my anxiety to make a friend,
even the few English words I knew by then flew out of my head,
and I responded in Yiddish. "Greenhorn," she taunted, her lips
curled in a sneer. "She's a greenhorn," she called to her friends
who ran to gather around. I didn't have to know the words; I had
only to look at the children's mocking smiles, at their faces filled
with scorn, to understand their meaning.

By the time my first year at school was over, I was well on my
way to fluency in my new language and refused to speak Yiddish
with my mother. She knew some English by then, but not enough
to make her way easily in the world. And it was many years before
she was comfortable enough in the language to become dominantly English-speaking. Meanwhile, my brother and I became
her teachers.

This reversal of roles—children as teachers—is one of the
more agonizing issues in immigrant family life. Talk about a generation gap! In immigrant families it's more like a canyon. As children become increasingly comfortable in the public world, they
not only distance themselves from the family culture, they become their parents' guides through the social and institutional
maze of the new land.

In my own family, my mother's illiteracy in any language
meant that her children were her surrogates in anything that required her to read and write. Over the years she made many attempts to become literate—the last when I was an adult and hired
a tutor to help her—all to no avail. It wasn't that she wasn't smart
enough. She was an intelligent woman with the kind of street
smarts that enabled her to work the system to her advantage when
she needed to. But the minute she took a pencil in her hand, her
anxiety rose to unmanageable levels and subverted her attempts

to learn. Consequently, my brother and I filled out her forms, checked her bills, told her the meaning of every communication she received, kept her abreast of important events. We were her eyes on the world.

But a child's help comes at a price. For the child who is also a parent's teacher is less likely to give unreflective assent to parental knowledge and authority—a shift in the dynamics of the family that's rarely spoken about but that's felt, even if not fully understood, by all. My mother, I'm certain, understood this all too well, and it made her a reluctant pupil.

It's nearly incomprehensible for those of us who take our literacy for granted to imagine a world where the letters on a page seem nothing more than gibberish, where something as simple as signing our name or reading a headline as we pass a newsstand is beyond our ability. That was my mother's universe, an internal world of pain and shame she could never escape. No wonder she would try any trick, make up any excuse ("I can't see to write this.") to conceal this most shameful of all her secrets. Or that she became so enraged at any reminder of it—reminders she couldn't escape when her children had to interpret every document that came to the house, fill out every form that required information.

I can still see those scenes: me at the table, a pen in my hand waiting for her to answer a question I'd read to her; she pacing the room angrily, the humiliation and frustration at not being able to do it herself too much to bear. "Write what I said," she would scream as she stood over me and pounded the table. Sometimes I could; at other times I wasn't able to because she couldn't or wouldn't give me the information necessary to answer the question properly. When I tried to explain what I needed, she stormed around furiously. "Educated dope," she'd shout at such moments, a gibe meant not just to wound me or put me in my place but to redress her humiliation and reclaim some knowledge and authority for herself.

I was reminded again of the anguish my mother's illiteracy cost her when I read Bernhard Schlink's powerful novel, *The Reader*. In it he tells the story of an illiterate woman who is charged with war crimes in a German court on the basis of a letter she couldn't possibly have written. Yet she remains mute, refusing to defend herself against the accusation because prison is preferable to the humiliation of exposing the secret of her illiteracy. My mother, I think, would have done the same.

Difficult as the reversal of roles between immigrant parents and their Americanized children is for the adults, they don't suffer it alone. It's equally fraught for the children. Until I became her guide in the public world, my mother seemed huge to me, a powerful woman whose word was law, even when I violated it; the woman who controlled my world, even when I fought her so tenaciously and won an occasional battle. When it became clear that there were important ways in which she couldn't navigate the larger world as well as I could, that changed. She seemed smaller, diminished—a vision that was at once relieving and frightening.

Given the difficulty of our relationship, there was something satisfying in seeing her cut down to size. But it was also anxiety-provoking because it shook my belief in her strength and power— a belief a child needs if she's to feel safe in the world. If my mother couldn't make her way comfortably in the world outside the family, if she spoke with an accent so that she wasn't easily understood, if she couldn't read and write, how could she provide the protection I needed?

Chapter Eight

My thoughts shift from past to present, from my mother to my daughter. It's nearly seven-thirty, time to call Marci and let her know I'm back and in the hospital. I know I should have called her yesterday, but at first I told myself I'd wait until I knew what was happening, then I couldn't make myself lay any more burdens on her when she was recovering from her own trauma. By the time I had a firm diagnosis and a phone from which to call, it was after eleven o'clock at night, too late for bad news. Now, as I dial her number, I'm a bit anxious about how she'll take the news. "Hi, Mom, where are you?" she asks when she hears my voice.

It feels as if we're in the middle of a soap opera. She, recovering from a cancer scare, is in pain from yesterday's surgery, which took a much larger chunk of her breast than expected. I, in my hospital bed with a life-threatening blood clot, now have to tell her my story. She gasps as she listens, interrupting me with questions. "Are you all right?" "How could you not call me?" "What does the doctor say?" "I can't believe you flew across the country when you knew you had a blood clot. How could you do that?"

We talk for a while, each trying to reassure the other, but neither of us is much comforted. She's upset because she can't move her arm well enough to drive herself to the hospital. "You don't have to rush over here; I'm not going anywhere," I tell her.

"Stop it, Mom," she commands impatiently. "I don't appreciate your trying to be so damned brave right now, and I'm really angry that all this was going on and you didn't let me know. I'll get Larry and be there as soon as I can."

I'm edgy and uncomfortable when we hang up. The fact is, I want to see her, and I'm upset with myself and my inability to say that to her. I understand that this is what comes of having had a mother who had such difficulty responding to her children's needs. I learned very early to keep my needs to myself, since their expression only brought more trouble, pain, and rejection. But my daughter isn't my mother, and Marci has never given me reason to believe she wouldn't be there for me if I asked. So my need to protect her, my inability to show my need fully to her, doesn't make sense, even to me.

My thoughts are interrupted by Hank's arrival. It's still early, but he has already canceled my patients for this week and returned the calls of friends who phoned yesterday. I listen as he fills me in on his various conversations, assuring me that he was careful to say nothing that would provoke any unnecessary anxiety in my patients. But I'm edgy waiting for Marci and Larry to arrive.

When they do, Larry greets me with a warm smile and stands aside as Marci walks tearfully into my arms. We hug each other gingerly; I, because I'm afraid to hurt her, she, as if fearful I might break. I pull back a bit to try to look at her, to see for myself how she's doing, but she's not ready to let go. We hold each other for a few minutes more, her tears dampening the fresh nightgown Hank just brought me. "I was so scared when you told me," she whispers into my shoulder. "I love you so much, Mom; you can't die, not yet, I'm not ready." After a while, we lean back and smile at each other through our tears. "Promise?" she says. "I promise."

Regaining her composure, she demands to know everything, probing for any detail or bit of information she thinks I might leave out. The intensity of her questioning makes me laugh, "You sound like a lawyer right now." "Well, I am a lawyer," she replies, unsmiling, "and this lawyer is pissed because you didn't call me right away."

We've had this conversation before. She insists she doesn't want to be protected from bad news; I resist delivering it to her. I keep thinking she ought to be glad that I want to protect her from unnecessary worry; she keeps telling me that she worries more because she's never sure she's hearing the whole story. I understand the words but I know it will be hard for me not to shield her, especially when I see her growing concern as we've gotten older.

We've had that conversation, too. We've been so close that I know my death will be a major blow to her. When I see evidence of her anxiety about my aging I try to keep it light. Sometimes I assure her jokingly that I won't die until she's ready; at other times, perhaps when she has admired some piece of jewelry I'm wearing, I'll say, "Glad you like it, but you'll have to wait a while to inherit it." She laughs at these moments, but usually ends such banter by telling me that she'll never be ready for me to die, that my death will "leave a hole in my heart that will never heal," and assures me also that she will survive and live well. This time, seeing her distress about not knowing, I tell her that I think I've finally gotten her message and promise not to withhold anything from her, now or in the future.

My heart swells with love for this child of mine, with gratitude for who she is and the great pleasure she has brought to my life. I remember the many times when I angered my mother for some crime I didn't even know I'd committed, remember her words, spit out like a curse, "I hope someday you'll have a daughter who's as rotten as you are, then you'll know how I feel."

"I won't," I'd mutter defiantly as I turned away to hide my pain. "I'll never be as mean to her as you are to me."

Now in the presence of my daughter's love, I'm filled with a sense of triumph. I did it; I broke the generational chain. I raised a daughter with whom I have a relationship built on mutual love, trust, and respect. I want to shake my fist at the heavens and shout, "See, I did it; I did what you couldn't do."

The day goes by in a blur of visitors and phone calls as the news of my whereabouts spreads among friends and colleagues. Hank, Marci, and Larry remain at my side until I finally send them away. I love them and appreciate their concern but it makes me edgy to watch them trying to make small talk while they anxiously scrutinize my every move.

I'm relieved to be alone again. I've finally allowed myself to feel the anxiety, and with it the exhaustion, of these last days. I push my bed down and lie back hoping to fall asleep. But my mind won't let me rest. I know this illness will change my life in some ways, but I don't yet know how. I'm accustomed to thinking of myself as healthy and fit, and I don't know where to put these feelings of fragility that now assault me.

I've always been an active person, driven some would say, and I can't imagine a life of curtailed activities. Both my mind and body move with the same quick impatience I saw in my mother and now see also in my daughter. I don't ride when I can walk; I don't sit still when I can move around; I don't slide by when pushing myself is an option. At the gym, where I have been working out for years, my new trainer is a Buddhist who laughs at what he calls my "type A personality" and reminds me every time I see him that I can get where I'm going just as fast if only I'd slow down a bit. I hear the words and appreciate the message, feeling intuitively that there's a profound truth in them. But until now, I've been emotionally incapable of moving from understanding to action.

I've been a psychotherapist for more than a quarter of a century, so I know that only in the movies is insight alone enough to bring about major personal change. I tell it to my patients often when, after months of examining the historical sources of some behavior that troubles them, they still say, "If I knew why maybe I could stop." The "why" question has an important place in the therapeutic process, of course, but there comes a moment when it also can be a way of avoiding the hard work of changing behavior.

Now as I contemplate the meaning of this illness, I ask myself, "Can I change?" Since my defensive system has largely served me well, I wonder, "Why would I want to?"

I've known for years that the intensity of engagement with which I approach all aspects of living has, at least in part, been in the service of warding off a depression that lies just below the surface. I've known, too, that I come by my depression naturally, since I've spent a lifetime watching both my mother and my brother dragged down into a depressive pit that ruined their lives. Which is why I'm so fearful of it in myself, why I often exhaust myself trying to hold it at bay.

Len, my brother, suffered depressions so severe that he was hospitalized and treated with electric shock therapy several times before he finally died in an automobile accident that looked more like a suicide. Like me, my mother warded off her depression by immersing herself in a busy daily life. The difference between us is only that my adaptation has been more functional than hers, perhaps because I had so many more options than she did. For her, there was no relief or pleasure in the busyness, no enjoyment in work she loved, no comfort in friends and family who care, only pain displaced by rage, an energizing emotion that swallowed up the ache of the sadness and allowed her to get out of bed in the morning and face each day anew.

Long before she died I thought often about the emotional suffering I knew she must have endured in her very difficult life. But I could never get her to talk about her feelings. I don't mean that she didn't gripe, complain, and criticize. Those were constant, whether about something or someone, me or my brother, or her life in general. And there was no dearth of self-pity in her verbal and emotional repertoire. But the kind of open revelation of herself—the kind of conversations I have with my husband, my friends, my daughter—this was never possible.

Even when my brother would sink into a vegetative depression from which he couldn't rouse himself, she couldn't allow herself to express her distress or to relate to his experience. It isn't that she was unconcerned; she was quite clearly very anxious about him. But instead of speaking her feelings she'd ask dismissively, as if he'd committed some crime, "What does he have to be depressed about?"

The first time I heard it, I thought this might be a serious question. But I was quickly disabused of the idea when she refused even to listen to anything I might say about his illness. "Never mind all your fancy talk; he gets moody because he thinks too much, that's all." *He thinks too much?* It was a bitter bad joke. My brother was one of the least reflective people I knew, and the idea that he "thinks too much" was so absurd I was rendered speechless.

Each time Len was hospitalized, I'd fly to New York; each time I arrived my mother and I would have the same fruitless conversations. I'd tell myself that I understood, that if she allowed herself to believe that my brother had a serious mental illness, she'd have to question the past, wonder about her mothering, ask what she might have contributed to his suffering, and perhaps worst of all, acknowledge her own depression. But it was hard to maintain my equilibrium in the presence of her anger and denial, and I'd become frustrated and lash out impatiently. "For God's sake; he's sick. Why are you so afraid to understand that? Didn't you ever feel depressed?"

She never looked at me at those moments; instead, she pushed my words away as if they were a physical force, "It's no use to think about the past; I just soldiered on. I didn't have time for such luxuries; I had to make a living for my children. He's weak, that's all; he always was." And with that she refused to talk further.

My heart shriveled when I heard her say such things. I understood then, as I do now, that there's a certain truth in what she said, that her life did, indeed, not allow her the luxury of sinking into a depression, and that the strength she displayed in allowing her, as she used to say, to "soldier on" was both extraordinary and commendable. But the cost . . . my God, the cost.

Chapter Nine

My father died in 1929, the year of the great stock market crash and the beginning of the worst depression the world had yet known. The rich were jumping from windows as they watched their fortunes melt away. The poor, accustomed to privation, plodded on stoically, a little poorer, a little hungrier, a little colder, a little more forlorn. In the midst of this social catastrophe stood my mother—twenty-seven years old, more than twenty years younger than my own daughter is now, a virtually penniless widow with two small children to support; a woman who was wholly illiterate, had no marketable skills, and spoke very little English.

It was easier then than it is now for a housebound immigrant woman to manage a life without English. The men, who had to make their way in the outside world, soon learned the language and became acculturated. But for a woman who didn't work outside the home, it was different. Television didn't exist; radios were a luxury out of the range of most poor immigrants. Even those who could afford one didn't have much incentive to buy a radio, since what poured forth from it sounded like so much noise to them. It was years later, after my brother and I had been in school for a while and had learned English well enough to care, that we agitated successfully for a radio.

The year or so following my father's death is a vague jumble in my mind, a time of blurred images seen as if through a misty fog.

What I remember most clearly is the word *yosem* (orphan), which is how the family referred to us among them selves. *"Oremer yo-semim"* (poor orphans), they'd say as they looked at us somberly, sending chills of apprehension through me. Why did they call us that? We weren't orphans; we had a mother. But she, too, talked about us as orphans. In fact, it was the big threat my mother held over our heads throughout our childhood. "Other mothers would have sent their children to the orphanage already," she'd cry when we displeased her, reminding us also that it was still not too late for her to do the same.

Although I've always known I was haunted by this fear, I never realized how deep-seated it was until my husband and I were traveling in Mexico a few years after we were married. There's a place in Guadalajara that has some murals by José Clemente Orozco, one of Mexico's great muralists, that I was eager to see. I knew before we went that the murals were in an orphanage, but I had managed to put that knowledge out of my mind by the time we got there. Or perhaps I assumed it was no longer used for that purpose. Whatever the reason, my denial was sustained by the fact that there were no children in sight when we arrived and were directed to the building with the murals. As we sat there marveling at the work before us, however, I began to feel a vague uneasiness stirring inside me, a restlessness that soon made it impossible to sit still.

I've often wondered what evoked my anxiety. Was it a child's voice heard only half consciously? I only know that one moment I had been gazing calmly at the beauty around me and the next I had an impulse to flee. After struggling unsuccessfully with it for a while, I turned to my husband and asked, "Can we go now?"

Surprised, he looked at me wonderingly and asked, "Anything wrong?"

"I don't know," I replied. "I just have to go."

We left the building and were walking across the grounds listening to the sound of church bells announcing the noon hour. As the last chime faded, the place exploded with children who poured from their classrooms and headed for lunch. I can still see them, perhaps a hundred children, chattering animatedly, some stopping to look at us, others to talk, while the nuns who cared for them urged them onward.

Yosemim, the word I would have sworn I'd forgotten, sprang instantly to mind. I found myself gasping for breath, my heart gripped by the same terror I'd felt as a child. I tried to pull myself back to adulthood, to speak to the children as they went by, to get some distance from the turmoil inside me. But all I could think of was *There but for the grace of God. . . .* In that moment, also, I felt that combination of anger and love, of aversion and admiration that characterized my feelings about my mother. For it wasn't by the grace of God but by her grace, and at some cost to herself, that my brother and I didn't share the fate of those children.

With my father's death our life in Philadelphia began to unravel. My mother looked for work, but there was nothing she could do except clean houses. In the deepening depression there wasn't much call for her services. At first the family gathered around offering what support they could. But my mother, whose fierce pride and independent spirit couldn't tolerate either a sense of helplessness or the idea that she was indebted to anyone, was soon engaged in a tragic reenactment of her past.

With resentments intensifying on both sides, my mother was once again banished from a family, only this time she was sent away with two small children. As she cast about desperately for alternatives, one of my father's brothers, who lived in New York City and remained distant from the strife between my mother and his family, urged her to come to New York and try her luck there. Within a year after my father's death, we moved away from the family and community I'd known all my life.

My mother left Philadelphia as she left the land and family of her birth, never to return or speak to any member of that family again. Forever after it was impossible to mention them without provoking her rage. *Far mir zien alla toit* (As far as I'm concerned, they're all dead), she'd answer furiously when I asked why she didn't talk to them anymore. *Zul zey brenen en drerd* (May they burn in hell), she'd say venomously when I wondered if we couldn't visit some of my cousins.

In New York we went to live in the Bronx with my aunt Lil and uncle Max, as mismatched a pair as anyone has ever seen. She was American-born, a mark of status to her; he was an unlettered immigrant. She was a small, trim person, *tidy* is the word that comes instantly to mind—a woman whose unaccented English, studied manners, and almost regal bearing claimed attention in the immigrant world in which we all lived. He was short and squat, a slovenly man whose crude vulgarity was designed to mock a wife who was always trying, in her words, "to elevate" her surroundings, which, he understood correctly, meant him above all. "Look at the American queen with the fleas in her nose," he'd taunt after he let go as loud a belch or a fart as he could muster. "She doesn't think anybody's good enough for her," he'd complain as he went by and pinched her backside or grabbed her breast while we watched.

She was an unhappy woman who had married for security and paid the price of living with a man she actively disliked. She was a misfit in her world, like a character in one of the Jane Austen novels she loved so much—a woman whose dreams went well beyond what was possible in her time and place. She was discontented with her life, contemptuous of her immigrant husband, and scornful of people she considered unmannered.

When I grew older, I'd wonder how they had managed to produce three sons, since it was impossible to imagine my aunt in a sexual embrace with her husband. But when I first met them I was too young for such speculation and too busy trying to fit into a new life to think much about anything else.

Although my uncle, who owned a butcher shop in Harlem, was one of the more affluent members of the tribe, space was tight in their apartment even without us. My youngest cousin, who was about two years old, slept in a crib in his parents' room. The two older boys—one the same age as my brother, the other closer to my age—slept in a room where only a child could pass comfortably between the wall and the bed they shared, which, after we arrived, accommodated my brother and me as well. Four small children sleeping crosswise on the bed.

We lived there for about six months during which time my

mother disappeared from our lives, a reality she refused ever to acknowledge. In fact, she was so intent on trying to wipe those months out of memory that, even in the face of my brother's and my active recollections, she not only denied she ever left but swore that we never lived in that household.

"But, Mom, I remember sleeping in the bed with the other kids and crying because you weren't there," I recall my brother insisting on one occasion.

For which he got a slap across the mouth and a furious, "You don't know anything. It never happened."

"You don't know anything!" "It never happened!" How often I heard those words when my version of reality differed from hers. How often I found myself questioning my sanity after she refused to acknowledge an event I knew had happened, whether something as big as living with Aunt Lil and Uncle Max or as small as a promise she made one day and failed to deliver on the next.

Later, as an adult, I spent many therapy sessions trying to sort out why I had trouble believing in my own experience. I'd recount an event to my therapist, then back off, uncertain about whether it had actually happened that way. "I think I embellish some of these stories because I like the drama and the attention they get me," I'd say to her. It took a long time before I came to understand that my questioning of myself was born of a childhood with a mother who so often turned reality on its head. That, and the fact that it's nearly impossible for a small child to believe fully that a parent—especially the only one—means to be hurtful or malevolent. Better to tell myself that I didn't understand, that it didn't happen that way, that I made the story up.

I see the same response among abused women and children in my clinical practice. Dependent upon their abuser, it's safer to blame themselves than the person who uses them badly. A little boy who's beaten up by his father consoles himself, "He just gets mad because I can't catch the ball the way he taught me." A woman nurses her bruises and explains, "He doesn't mean it. It's just that I couldn't stop the baby from crying and it made him crazy. I know he loves me; he's always sorry afterward."

Even now what my brain understands my heart doesn't always

get, and cognitive knowledge isn't translated into emotional certainty. On those occasions when a friend and I come up with different versions of the same event, I still turn inward to question myself: Did it really happen? Did I get it right, or is it my mistake? And I still sometimes need an outside arbiter to help me figure out what's true—a role my husband, Hank, has played for most of our marriage. For years I never phoned my mother without asking him to listen in on the extension. It was a rare conversation when I didn't have some reason to ask afterward, "Did she really say that or am I making it up?"

Doubts assail me as I write this book as well. Each time I tell a "bad mother" story on these pages, I have to stop and ask myself, "Are you sure you're not exaggerating? Was it really that bad, or have you embellished it because it makes a better story this way?" After weeks of grappling by myself with my questions and misgivings, I tell Hank. "I worry that I'm making her worse than she was."

Once again he steps into the role of truth teller, reminding me of all the other times when I struggled with my uncertainties needlessly. I listen to his reassurances, to his reminders of who my mother was, what he witnessed with his own eyes and ears, and want urgently to believe him and thus believe myself. But the doubts creep back in.

The same anxieties plague me socially, albeit in less intense form. If someone is ten minutes late for an appointment, I begin to fret: Did I get the time right? The day? Am I in the right place? Maybe she meant the restaurant where we met last time? Maybe something happened, and he can't reach me to say he isn't coming? The depth of my relief when they finally show up, as they always do, is testimony to the irrational intensity of my doubts.

I used to wonder how old I'd have to be before my brain and my emotional response were in synchrony, before I could believe fully in what I know, in the validity of my own experience. But the irony, I now find, is that at just the time when I might expect the years to have loosened the hold of the past, age has taken its toll on memory and there are new reasons to question what I know.

Now, when a friend recently insisted, "No, don't you remember I said we couldn't have dinner with you before the concert?" it wasn't only the experiences of my youth but the memory failures of age that made me question my own recollection.

My mother's disappearance, coming as it did on the heels of my father's death and our move from Philadelphia, left my brother and me terrified. Where did she go? When will she be back? What will happen to us if she doesn't come home? I can still see my brother sitting on the floor in a corner of my aunt's tiny kitchen, his arms hugging his drawn-up knees, his quavering voice repeating over and over again, "Where's Mommy? I want Mommy." For a long time, I clung to my aunt as if for life, trying never to let her out of my sight, feeling frightened nearly to the point of panic whenever I couldn't be close to her.

The fear of abandonment that still can grip me with dread without much provocation is the legacy of those years. If my husband is a half hour late getting home, my anxieties soar. I tell myself he's fine, that he's been delayed because an appointment took longer than expected, because traffic slowed him down. But no words can touch the terror I feel, the conviction that something terrible has happened, that any minute the police will show up at my door to tell me he's dead.

At this late stage of my life, I get exasperated with myself when these ancient anxieties come to the fore. I want to shake myself and shout: 'Enough! Get over it!" I laugh as those words come to mind, knowing I sound very much like my mother. But I also ask, "Is it really so unreasonable to expect that at seventy-three I would have learned not to let these old experiences color my life today?" The therapist in me knows the answer; reason has nothing to do with it. But the woman who has endured these abandonment fears from childhood into old age wants them to stop.

I don't know if my aunt and uncle knew where my mother had gone or why. They never said, not then nor at any time afterward. While we were there our questions were met with words meant to reassure us that she would return soon. Afterward, when my mother kept denying it had ever happened, I asked my aunt about it. She confirmed my memory and with it affirmed for me that I wasn't crazy. In adulthood I came to believe my mother had given way to some kind of a desperate impulse to run from the life that was threatening to overwhelm her. But no matter how hard I've tried, I've never been able to imagine what she did or how she lived during those months.

I was awed by Aunt Lil, who was the only American-born adult in the family, the only one I'd met until then, since I hadn't yet started school when we left Philadelphia. Although she only finished the eighth grade before she had to leave school to help support her family, it was a high accomplishment in that milieu, more than enough to set her apart from the rest of my aunts and uncles, few of whom had any formal education at all.

Until we went to live with Aunt Lil, I never saw a book in anyone's house; I didn't know a library existed; no one had ever read me a story. It didn't seem strange then; it was just the way it was. Many years later when I was doing the research for *Worlds of Pain,* one of my early books on working-class family life, most of the homes I went into were like the one I grew up in, no books around, no good light to read by, except that by then a large color TV dominated the room.

In my aunt's presence, the narrow, cloistered world I'd lived in began to give way. It was as if the doors of my mind swung open to a wonderful world of possibilities I couldn't even dream of before. Where my mother hunkered down behind closed doors, real and metaphorical, my aunt searched life out, even if only in books. I loved everything about her—her quieter ways, her more refined manner, her melodious voice, her knowledge of books, the sound of her native speech. I wanted to be just like her. By the time my mother came back, I was firmly attached to Aunt Lil and had convinced myself that I would stay there forever as her adopted daughter. A fantasy aided and abetted by my aunt who saw in me the little girl she longed for and hadn't been able to produce.

It's one of the strange, paradoxical realities of my life that my mother's departure, frightening though it was, opened the door to a relationship with my aunt that might not have been possible otherwise. During the months we lived there, she was my lifeline, the adult I came to depend on, the one I had to believe in if I was to survive, and, most important perhaps, the woman I admired more than any I'd met until then. I could adopt her as the model of what I wanted to be without feeling guilty about abandoning my mother because she had already forsaken me.

My brother had a different experience. It wasn't that my aunt and uncle weren't kind to him, too. But in my mother's house he had been the one who had been singled out as special; in this family he was just another boy in a household that already had three others. That, coupled with the fact that he was more emotionally identified with my mother than I was, made her disappearance much harder for him than it was for me. Throughout all our months there, he never stopped talking about her, wondering where she was, waiting anxiously for her return. Finally she did, relieving my brother greatly but leaving me conflicted between my joy in knowing that she cared enough to come back and the knowledge that we'd have to leave my aunt's house, the first loving home I'd ever known.

Chapter Ten

I feel as if I've been in the hospital for a month but it's only three days and there are still four more to go. Even with lots of visitors and phone calls, the days are long here. I have books to read and work to do, but a hospital is no place for rest, relaxation, or work. Every time I think I can finally settle down and concentrate, someone comes in to do something to or for me.

My doctor tells me that he'll probably let me walk around tomorrow, but where can I go tethered, as I am, to an IV? "If I can walk around, why can't I go home?" I want to know. It seems ridiculous to be spending day and night in a hospital bed when I have no obvious signs of illness. "I'll not only be better off at home," I tell him, "but we'll be doing our share to keep medical costs down." He laughs, but shakes his head. I remind him that Hank was a premed student in his earlier life and was in the medical corps in a couple of wars. He could easily learn how to keep tabs on the IV, and if that didn't work, we could get a home nursing service to come in and do what's necessary. But he tells me I'm not out of the woods yet, that I need to be where skilled medical people are available in case of an emergency.

I know I'm defeated, but I don't feel much like giving way gracefully, so I say good-bye to him without my usual warm thanks for the attentive care he's given me. It isn't just the tedium of the days that's so hard; bad as that is, it's easier than the nights where my dreams don't allow oblivion.

It's early in the morning and I'm running lightly and easily down a familiar path near the bay. At this hour, with the sun still rising in the east and casting a pink and golden glow in the western sky, the Golden Gate Bridge seems particularly well named. Suddenly an old crone, her wrinkled, toothless face fixed in a horrible grin, appears before me. She looks vaguely familiar but I can't figure out why. I shudder uncomfortably and back away a few steps, but she stays right with me. I try to run around her but she blocks my way. Frustrated, I push her aside, but she bounces back like one of those weighted toys that you can't knock over no matter how hard you hit it.

"What do you want?" I shout. "Who are you?" But before the question is out of my mouth, I know the answer. She's death. I try again to push her away, but she doesn't move. I'm frightened but try to hide it. I want to shout at her, to tell her that she doesn't scare me, that I'm not afraid of her, but no matter how hard I try, no words will come. She laughs, a terrible cackle, and turns away and disappears.

I awaken feeling puzzled and alarmed. The dream seems so obvious, yet it doesn't make sense. I don't feel afraid of dying. When I was on that plane and knew I could die, I never felt fear, only sadness for my loved ones. Whatever mild apprehension I may have felt was overpowered by the much stronger feeling that this was as good a way as I could imagine to go into the still dark night. So why now do I awaken from a dream of death dancing before me feeling so agitated?

The dream stays with me all morning until Kim calls and I recount it to her. She thinks for a moment, then says, "Maybe you've interpreted the dream too literally and have misidentified the old crone. It seems to me she isn't death but your fear of old age."

I go back to the feelings in the dream and remember my sense that the old woman was familiar. The reinterpretation seems exactly right: I was looking in the mirror; that repugnant old crone was a vision of my future, who I am to become. I shudder. "Yes, that's it, of course, an ugly old age that's no different from my mother's."

Kim and I talk for a few more minutes, but I'm eager to get off the phone and deal with my feelings. My mother's death has had the peculiar effect of throwing me back to my past and into my future at the same time. So I keep rummaging around in my childhood looking for something, some way to package my past with her while I search for reassurance that my future will be different from hers. If anyone had asked me before she died, I would have said that I long ago made peace with my mother, that I had bundled her up with good hunks of my past and stowed it all neatly in the back of my memory closet. Now, as I wrestle with the reality that she has once again become a looming presence in my internal life, I know I was wrong. It's as if her death has brought me to the final showdown with both past and future.

My thoughts wander back to my dream and the old crone and I understand better why I'm more upset by seeing her as my aging self than when I thought she was death. Whether in childhood or old age, my determination—no, my need—to be different from my mother, to live my life differently, to see myself and be seen differently, has been a driving force.

But that's not all. I know there's something more, something that I can't yet see that dismays me so about this dream. I lie back on my bed and try to let my mind roam free, to feel my way into awareness. Immediately the word *shame* pops into my head. Shame? Yes, there it is. I'm ashamed to be old, ashamed that the day may not be far off when others will look at me as I looked at her.

Getting old in our society is distasteful and difficult, not just because of our own fears of aging and death but because of the social stigma that clings to old age. As a worker in a nursing home commented wryly in a *New York Times* article on the elderly, "These survivors . . . win no honor from a society that promotes longevity but at the same time denies death and shuns its emissaries, the frail elderly. 'I see people back away from them when we go on trips.' "

We're uncomfortable about our feelings—the old are, after all, our parents and grandparents—so we look away. We don't even use the word *old* anymore; instead we now talk about *senior citizens*—a label that, as Mary-Lou Weisman writing in the *New York*

Times recently argued, "while intending to reconfer respect, instead made a senior citizen sound like an over-decorated captain in 'The Pirates of Penzance.' " Yet most old people grasp eagerly at the designation in the vain hope that by changing the name they'll change the reality.

But whatever we call them, our feelings are the same: We don't like old people, find little use for them, and would, if we could, hide them all away in what we euphemistically call *retirement communities* where we wouldn't have to see them and would, therefore, be spared a confrontation with our own future. That's better, I suppose, than Anthony Trollope's futuristic vision in his novel *The Fixed Period,* where he foresaw a society that would send its old to a place where they could enjoy a year of contemplation, after which they would be dispatched by chloroform to a peaceful death.

It's not a surprise, therefore, that we who are old or on the brink of it find many ways to deny the fact. I had a conversation recently with a woman a couple of years older than I who, although hobbled by arthritis, lamented the disparity between the state of her body and her internal sense of herself. "My body may be crippled and old, but inside me I don't feel any different than I always did."

It's a common fantasy. For years, I, too, felt that the inside and outside were mismatched. I understand the unconscious impulse behind such denial: If we nourish the conviction of a discrepancy between the outside and the inside, clutch it closely to our bosom, we're more able to sustain the belief that they "out there" see the inside at least as clearly as the outside. For me that illusion was swept away with my mother's death and my pulmonary embolus, coming as it did just days after my seventy-third birthday. I don't mean that I suddenly feel old and incompetent, only that now, for the first time, my internal sense of myself matches the years I've marked off on life's calendar.

The phone rings and interrupts my thoughts. It's Riese, a close friend with whom I also share my clinical office. She has an unexpected cancellation and, since our office is just a few blocks from the hospital, she wants to drop by. I'm delighted. I've had enough of my brooding, enough of trying to figure out how to grow old gracefully, enough of my own company.

While I wait I think about how important this woman has been in my life for the last dozen years or so, how much our lives have become entwined, what an enjoyable foursome Hank and I and she and Bill have become. We've shared holidays, hiked over the hills and valleys in the Dordogne, tasted the wines of the Napa Valley, sat over innumerable dinners in restaurants from San Francisco to New York to Paris.

My thoughts bring me up short again. I can't think, let alone write, about my life now without wanting to explain, to wave my hand and shout, "Wait, hold on, don't judge me. I haven't forgotten how far I've come from my roots; I know how privileged I am." In fact, I rarely leave or enter the building I live in without some note of discord jostling my mind, without some internal reminder that it's a long way from New York's urban immigrant ghetto to San Francisco's Nob Hill.

Riese arrives smiling broadly and bearing a beribboned basket of goodies, her trademark gift. She doesn't have much time, so we spend it catching up, not that I've been doing anything that merits telling. Although the face she shows me is smiling warmly, I see the concern in her lovely dark eyes. Finally, she reaches for my hand, takes it in hers, and asks, "Are you okay?"

I know she doesn't mean my physical condition alone. I shrug, trying to hold back the tears her question evokes. "I don't know yet" is all I can say.

Her presence has been comforting, and I'm saddened when she looks at her watch and realizes she must run. We kiss good-bye, and I probably hold on to her a little tighter than usual. She pulls back, looks at me, then hugs me tightly one last time as we both try to lighten the moment with cheery farewells that neither of us feels.

I lean back and stare at the ceiling for a while before picking up a book and trying to read. But my mind won't settle down to the words on the page. I turn on the TV and channel surf, but nothing captures my attention. Finally I open my laptop computer, which Hank brought to me this morning, and try to work on the concluding chapter of the book I've been writing. It's called *The Transcendent Child*—eight stories of men and women who have transcended difficult and painful childhoods, usually in the way their siblings have not.

All my work, from the first book to the last, started with some interest that grew out of the issues in my own life. It doesn't take any psychological sophistication to know what brought me to my research into transcendent children. I have lived with a lifetime of guilt and wonder at being the child who made it, the one who overcame the deficits of our past when my brother could not. "Why me and not him?" I asked myself a thousand times as I watched his painful and often failed struggle to manage his life successfully. The manner of his death, the way he chose to depart from this earth, haunted me enough to send me searching once again for some answers, this time in the lives of others as well as my own.

From the time my father died, my brother suffered a variety of mysterious physical ailments (the most visible being a tick, an involuntary twisting of his neck and head accompanied by a thrust of a leg) that were never clearly diagnosed but that left him unable to function very well from time to time. I know now that many, if not all, of his problems were psychosomatic—real illnesses with real symptoms, but maladies that were complicated by psychological issues, if not actually psychological in origin.

My relationship with my brother was complicated, not just by his infirmities and my jealousy of the attention he got but by our differences in temperament and in gifts. From our earliest childhood, his pessimism and my optimism stood in opposition to one another. Where he saw darkness and danger, I saw opportunity and excitement. We were both our mother's children. But he took from her her fears; I took her determination. Anxiety and dread were his constant companions—terrors that, in adulthood, sometimes sent him into depressions that were severe enough to require hospitalization and that finally killed him.

My dominant childhood memory of our relationship is of his teasing me mercilessly, which sometimes brought me to tears and at other times found me chasing after him furiously, often with a kitchen knife in my hand. When I try to recall now just what made me so angry, I can't find the content, only the feeling. I used to think it was a miracle that I didn't kill him or, at the very least, wound him seriously. Now I'm certain it wasn't an accident that I never caught him in one of those chases. My rage frightened me as much as it did him, and I don't think I was eager to test out the limits to which it would take me.

Mostly as we grew into our middle years, we didn't have much to do with each other, which is why he seems like such a cipher in this story. He was always out on the street; I was always buried in a book. Like my mother, he couldn't tolerate my withdrawal into my own world and taunted me repeatedly about thinking I was "better than everybody else around." Which only made me withdraw further.

Yet we weren't all distance and conflict. Although we never had any common interests and not much to talk about, we were aware of the bond between us, that mystical bond of family that knows no explanation. True, it was an ambivalent attachment we had to one another, but it bound us together throughout our lives. While, as a child, I was envious and resentful of the attention he got by being sick, I also saw him as fragile and in need of protection. Often, therefore, when my mother's wild rage was directed at him, I'd try to deflect it to me, certain that I was better able to stand up to her than he was.

On his side, although he was obsessed with money to the point of miserliness, he would occasionally buy me what in our world were extravagantly expensive gifts—things like the bowknot birthstone ring I coveted that cost $8, which was a fortune in our family. In fact, I was the only one in his life, including later his wife and children, who was ever the beneficiary of any largesse from him.

Even as a child I wondered about his generosity with me, especially when he didn't complain very loudly when I stole some of the tips he earned for delivering groceries. He accused; I denied. But we both knew I'd taken the money, and he never retaliated. Nor did he put his money in a less easily accessible place to prevent the thefts, or at least to slow them down. Instead, he left it in a box in plain sight on top of the dresser in the bedroom my mother and I shared.

Later, when I learned more about family dynamics, I thought about the sexual tinge in our relations with each other. As children there was an intensity between us that was evident whenever we came together, whether in a rare moment of amity or in conflict. Not surprising, I suppose, since we were alone so much, slept in the same room for years, and, in many ways, were so dependent on each other.

The one time in his life when my brother touched his real potential, when he felt competent and masterful, was in the army during World War II. Without warning he announced one evening that he had enough of his college deferment and was going to enlist the next day. I expected my mother to go berserk, but instead she sent him off without a twinge, convinced that he'd be rejected for reasons of health. "With his heart and that tick, who's going to take him in the army?" she asked rhetorically as she closed the door behind him and, with a self-satisfied smile, prepared to leave for work herself.

But the army didn't agree. By nightfall he was back with orders to report to Fort Dix in New Jersey for induction the next day. "They said there's nothing wrong with me, and I have to leave tomorrow," he announced proudly as if he'd won some kind of a contest.

Even then I think I dimly understood that this was, in fact, an important victory for him, the first big step in what would become his lifelong and largely unsuccessful attempt to sever the hostile symbiotic relationship in which he and my mother were locked. At the moment, however, I could only watch horrified as my mother collapsed onto the floor, keening and tearing her hair. My brother went to comfort her, to help her off the floor, and it looked for a moment as if he might calm her. But as she rose to her feet, she shoved him away and ran out the door screaming invective at God, at the army, at anyone she held responsible for taking her son from her.

My brother left the next day, and I was surprised at my distress. I wept as I walked with him to the subway station and waited for the train that would take him away. I was scared that he wouldn't be able to cut it as a soldier, that I couldn't protect him, that he'd die with no one there to comfort him.

It didn't work that way. He stood the test of war far better than anyone, including him, would have imagined, and his years in the army were the best and most successful of his life. Once he got away from my mother, he left behind the weak and sickly definition with which he had been tagged since early childhood. Even the tick that had plagued him through most of his life disappeared. For those few short years, he tapped parts of himself he hadn't known before, became the man he wanted to be, and acquitted himself on the battlefields of Germany with honor—a matter of pride for him until the day he died. Unfortunately, once home, he moved quickly back into the old relationship with my mother, and his newly emerging self slipped quietly away. Within weeks of his return from the army, the tick reappeared, and the first signs of serious depression emerged. He could fight Hitler but couldn't stand up to my mother.

With these thoughts rattling around in my head, I turn my attention back to my computer and try to write for a while. But my memories continue to intrude as my mind wanders again to the past I shared with my brother and to the time when my mother reappeared as suddenly as she had left six months earlier.

It was common in those years for poor immigrant families to take in lodgers or boarders, or for one poor family to rent space to another. So when my mother returned, we moved into a series of apartments that were already too small for the family that lived there. Although they weren't in the back of a store, like the one we lived in with my father, they were the same kind of flats, designed so that all the rooms were off a long, narrow hall. Sometimes there was a bathroom in the apartment; sometimes it was in the hall outside. My mother, brother, and I lived and slept in one of the rooms and had what were called *kitchen privileges*. Which meant my mother was allowed some space in the icebox and could cook our meals at specified times.

I still recoil when I think of those overcrowded, dark, and dingy places—the noise, the smells, the fights, sometimes in the other family, sometimes between them and my mother. We never stayed anywhere more than a couple of months, sometimes because she fell out with the host family, sometimes because someone offered a better deal, sometimes for no reason other than her need to keep moving. Whatever her reasons, the new place was never any different from the one we'd just left. "Why do we have to move again?" I'd cry when my mother started to pack us up.

"Stop crying or I'll give you something to cry about" was all the answer I ever got.

It wasn't until a year or so later, when my mother found her way into New York's garment industry, that we finally got an apartment of our own. The building we moved into—one of the many dreary, redbrick, six-story walk-up buildings that lined the Bronx neighborhoods we lived in—was no different from the ones we left when we lived with others. Our apartment was on the fourth floor, a tiny one-room studio with a bed in one wall, a cramped little kitchenette along another, our very own bathroom, and a window that faced a brick wall so close you could almost reach out and touch it. It was dark and cold in the winter, dark and hot in the summer, but it was ours. My mother and I slept in the bed; my brother was on a cot. I was seven years old.

Later, when I was eleven and my brother nearly thirteen, my mother decided we should no longer sleep in the same room, and we moved to a one-bedroom apartment, the only one of our many moves I ever appreciated. After years in a single room, an apartment with a real kitchen, a living room, and a bedroom felt nearly palatial to me. For the first time, it was possible to find a corner where I could retreat behind my ever-present book without being in sight and sound of my mother, without having to listen to her complain, "You think you're smarter than everybody else with your nose always stuck in a book."

As always, it wasn't long before that apartment gave way to another one just like it. It was many years before I came to understand that, while my mother's restless searching for something I'm sure she couldn't have named played a central part in the peripatetic life we led, there was another piece to the story. Depression-strapped landlords, hungry for tenants to fill their vacant apartments, offered one month's free rent to anyone willing to sign a year's lease. By moving every year, therefore, she not only momentarily assuaged her restlessness but saved a full month's rent.

I must have fallen asleep because when I open my eyes Marci is sitting and reading next to my bed. The sight of her lifts my mood and we talk for a half hour or so before she has to get back to work. When she's gone, I look around the room, which is no longer the barren box it was when I first arrived. Plants and flowers fill every surface, get well balloons hang from the ceiling, and several boxes of my favorite chocolates sit on a table in the corner. At the side of my bed are about a dozen books, some brought by friends, others by Marci. Our reading tastes are much the same and we're always exchanging books, from the junk mysteries we gobble up to the more literary novels we love.

Looking at this evidence of the love and warmth of friends and colleagues, I feel deeply privileged. And I wonder, as I often do: How did I get from there to here? How did that lonely isolated child who had so little talent for friendship grow up to such a rich social life?

"Teacher's pet," my classmates called me through most of my years in grade school. They weren't wrong. My academic successes coupled with my infatuation with my teachers, who took their place beside Aunt Lil as the embodiment of what I wanted to be, made me a great favorite with them. But while their admiration and approval were a balm to my troubled young soul, it wasn't without a cost. It isolated me from the other kids and underscored my alienation as well as the lonely realization that I wasn't very good at friendship.

In this, I was indeed my mother's daughter, partly, I suppose, because I had no model of how to make and keep a friend. Her ability to carry a grudge, to clasp old angers to her heart as if letting them go might endanger her, was striking. I can understand it intellectually: Anger was her weapon against her own softer side, against being inundated by her hurts and her vulnerability. For both good and ill, it was the energizing force in her life, the force that propelled her forward, that enabled her to survive and to overcome the difficulties that were set before her. But emotionally, holding grudges like that will never make any sense to me.

In all the years I lived with my mother, I never saw her make and keep a friend. It wasn't as if she had no opportunities. She had co-workers and neighbors who would have been likely candidates. But the few times she allowed anyone to come near, the relationship quickly foundered on her paranoid vision. She was quick to take umbrage at any slight, real or imagined, and neither explanation nor apology brought forgiveness. Instead, she'd fall into a mean-spirited rage and banish the offender forever.

I never shared my mother's paranoia, in that I didn't assume that others were deliberately out to get me. But it's hard when you grow up in a household where your only parent saw everyone who crossed her path as a potential threat to feel at ease with others. It's hard, too, when you feel like the alien other in that family, to believe you can belong anywhere, and harder still, when your own mother doesn't like you, to believe others will.

I think, too, that I'd become so accustomed to my isolation that I didn't know how to be a friend. The cooperation, the give and take, the mutual sharing friendship requires—all these were alien to me then. Moreover, I wasn't interested in the things the other little girls held so dear, and I didn't try to be. Like dolls. I couldn't understand their fascination with dolls, why they'd want to spend endless hours dressing and undressing them, pretending they were mommies and these were their babies.

Now I can ask myself, "Was it that I really didn't like to play with dolls or was this my defense against the fact that I never had one? Or was my distaste for doll play rooted in my experience with my mother?" Now I believe that for a little girl to want to play the nurturing mommy to her doll baby, she needs to have been adequately mothered herself. Then my lack of interest in dolls just seemed to be one more reason why I had trouble making friends.

But even when I made a friend it was hard to sustain the relationship because we kept moving house every year. It may seem odd now, when parents make play dates for their children with friends who live some distance away, that moving a few blocks would mean the end of a friendship. But in the Bronx of that era, children's social life was lived on the block, and moving even a short distance was a major upheaval, especially during the elementary school years.

For my brother and me, therefore, each move meant that we were once again the new kids on the block, trying to find our way into a street world that had been doing just fine without us. Sometimes the moves were close enough to keep us in the same school; most of the time they meant both a new school and a new neighborhood.

My brother managed these moves somewhat better than I did, partly because of the gender differences in the way children play. Boys are more apt to move about in groups, to play games that call for a team; girls are more likely to form dyads, intimate little twosomes that exclude all others. He ran off to play stickball, or whatever other game they were playing, welcomed by the other boys so long as he could hit the ball well enough to help the team. I stood in front of our building, sometimes for hours, watching the other girls hungrily, hoping someone would notice, would talk to me, would invite me into a game of jump rope or hopscotch. Eventually someone did. But by the time I found a friend and acceptance on the street, we were on the move again.

Later, in junior high and high school, when students were more mobile and also were drawn from a wider geographic area, moving didn't present such a formidable obstacle to forming friendships. And while I was somewhat more successful then, my self-consciousness and fears of exposure kept me from becoming a part of any group.

Adding to my problems in making friends was the fact that, in those days, the only thing the New York City schools could think to do with very bright children was to let them skip grades. From first to sixth grade, therefore, I skipped two full years, one reason no doubt for the arithmetic lapses—long division and fractions in particular—that remain with me to this day. The third skipped year came in junior high, where a program for gifted children allowed me to do the seventh and eighth grades in one year instead of two.

When I entered high school in the ninth grade, therefore, I was two to three years younger than my classmates, a gap so wide at that age that it would have been a tough challenge for a child far more socially skilled than I was. For me, it was an unbridgeable chasm. No matter which way I turned, I couldn't find a place where I fit. Intellectually I was too far ahead of children my own age; socially and emotionally I was too far behind the classmates who should also have been my peers.

A knock on the door interrupts my thoughts. It's Michael, an intimate friend whom I met when I asked him to serve on my dissertation committee thirty years ago. He was a young assistant professor in political science at the time, a man with radical politics and a quirky, brilliant mind that awed me then, still does at times. He had published a fascinating book on the role of intellectuals in the McCarthy era— arguably the best work ever written on the subject—and since politics (school busing, in particular) was the subject of my work, I was eager to have his advice and support.

Now, from my hospital bed, I watch him walk toward me, his faced etched with concern, and I wonder about the mysterious chemistry that draws people together. When we met, Michael was a thirty-year-old man whose first child hadn't yet been born; I was the forty-five-year-old mother of one of his undergraduate students, although I don't think he knew that then. An unlikely combination for the kind of lasting friendship that grew quickly out of our work together. It's true that Michael and I shared a deep connection to the politics of the time and the history that got us there, but that was true of others I knew as well. Yet it's we two who sit in this hospital room thirty years later, talking about the

past, worrying about the future, marveling at the history of inti-
macies, ideas, politics, and intellectual work we've shared, knowing that this connection between us will endure for a lifetime.

When he leaves I think about my closest friends, wondering if
there's a single common quality that sparked and now sustains the
friendship. The one thing that rings true is that, despite great
differences in their personal styles and their personalities, despite
their often large successes in the external world, internally all of
them feel themselves to be marginal, to live outside the mainstream, often even in those arenas where they have made their
mark. What's it like, I wonder, to have been the prom queen or the
captain of the football team? No one in my close personal circle
will ever know.

The prom queen! As a child I would have settled for a few
friends. Or at least that's what I thought at the time. Looking back
now, I know that, distressing as my marginality was, much as I
wanted to feel part of a group, my experience with my mother
taught me to value my separateness, to embrace it as I searched for
a self that was independent of another's definition of me. I didn't
like being the misfit, in the family or anywhere else, but I liked
even less the threat to my integrity that belonging seemed to
promise. So I remained apart, a child who was in the world but not
of it, the one who was the observer of life rather than a participant
in it. After a while, I was so accustomed to being left out—and to
leaving myself out—that it was hard for me to come in even when
I was invited.

It's still true today. Although in adulthood I developed a finely
honed capacity for friendship and have had intimate and long-
lasting friendships throughout my adult life, I've never experienced myself as an insider, never comfortably belonged to a group,
whether in my personal or professional life. In my private life, my
friends have been drawn from worlds so distant that they usually
didn't know each other until I brought them together. In the professional world, I span two disciplines—sociology and psychology—and don't feel wholly at home in either one. And although
I complain about that from time to time, I don't jump at the
chance to belong when it's offered to me.

When, for example, I was invited to apply for a professorship at Harvard some years ago, I was pleased and gratified to know that my work had been noticed and appreciated. But I was also anxious, because being "in" was not only an alien experience but an unsettling one. Just contemplating the possibility took me back to my childhood, to the moments when it seemed to me that to be a real part of my family I had to give up my soul. I knew once again the visceral fear of fitting in, the vague but powerful sense that to belong would be to lose myself—feelings that lay right alongside the equally disturbing possibility that I *couldn't* fit in, that if I accepted, they'd surely find a way to reject me.

I refused the invitation. To accept it was too risky, too profoundly at odds with my belief that my autonomy, as well as my intellectual and creative capacities, were deeply linked to being an outsider.

Chapter Eleven

It's day seven of my hospital stay, the day I'm supposed to go home. Hank arrived early this morning, and we're waiting for my doctor to come and sign me out. But when he walks into the room I know at once there's trouble. No matter how carefully they calibrate the dosage, my pro time continues to swing wildly between dangerously high and alarmingly low. "I can't let you go home yet," he tells me, looking almost as sad as I feel.

A lump rises in my throat, choking off my breath, and my eyes swim with unshed tears. I feel foolish, like a disappointed child who wants to weep and shout, "But you promised." Instead, I ask, "How much longer?" knowing before the words are out of my mouth that he doesn't know. He shrugs; it happens sometimes, not often, but it happens. It's nothing to be concerned about, he assures me, they'll get it under control. Neither of us knows yet that I'll never have a two-week period when my pro time isn't either too high or too low. Now, however, I can't help wondering why, if there's nothing to fear, he looks so worried.

When the doctor leaves Hank and I sit holding hands and staring out the window. What is there to say? I can feel myself sinking into depression, and I know he is, too. I want to lighten the mood, but my head is filled with morbid thoughts about aging and dying. I don't know what else to do, so I call Marci, as promised, to let her know I won't be going home. I can hear in her voice that she's upset and frightened, but she tries for the light touch. "Well, I guess you're not ready to give up all the attention yet, are you?" Our laughter isn't very convincing to either of us, so she finally asks, "Are you scared?"

"Yes," I say, "but not of dying. I'm scared that this damn thing will change my life and curtail my activities. I can't bear the thought of an infirm old age."

"Mom, I know you don't believe it now, but you'll never be infirm; it's not your style."

It's a child's wishful thinking, no doubt, but the words soothe me for a moment. We talk a few minutes more and hang up after she promises to come by after work.

I'm still sad and frightened, but my mood is lighter, if also a little macabre, so I turn to Hank and say, "If this thing kills me, I want a big memorial service where everyone I care about comes to say how wonderful I was."

He laughs, "I thought we both decided we didn't want any of that nonsense."

"That was before I really thought I'd die. I have to admit, I'd rather have it while I'm still alive and can hear what people say, but since that's not the way it works, I'll take it when I'm dead."

"Guess what," he says, "you don't have to die. I'll be happy to arrange it for you while you're still around."

We're quiet for a few moments, each with our own thoughts. Then, "What are you thinking?" I ask.

"I'm trying to get used to the idea that you might die, and I don't think I can."

Usually we talk easily about our impending decline and death, but I don't want to have a serious conversation now, not when decline, if not death, is right in my face. So I smile and reply lightly, "Think of it this way, when I'm gone you'll never have to make the bed again," referring to the fact that he hates to put the top quilt on the bed every day.

It's one of our little jokes as we try to cope with the inevitable, to find ways to deal with what we're so afraid to confront. It helps us to feel that we have some control, somewhat like my suicidal fantasies earlier in my life. For while Hank doesn't particularly fear his own death either, we each tremble at the idea of living without the other. So I tell him that my one consolation will be that I can take over his bookshelves in our shared office. He says he'll move into my desk, which has the better view of the Golden Gate Bridge.

It's close to ten by now, and this is one of the three mornings a week when Hank teaches at a high school in the city. He thought he'd be able to get me home in time to get to his ten-thirty class, but now he reaches for the phone to say he won't be there. I stop him. I know he'll feel better if he goes, and there's not much reason for him to hang around here. Besides, if he's not here maybe I can distract myself with a book or some work. Reluctantly, he agrees, promising to be back by one with a special lunch.

The phone rings; it's Diane, the woman I think of as my "all-purpose" friend because she's so firmly integrated into every aspect of my life—personal, professional, and trivial. Yes, trivial, like shopping, one of life's many necessities at which she's expert, although I doubt she'd agree that it's a trivial pursuit. When I need a bathing suit, I take Di, who astounds me when we walk into Macy's, with its array of twenty or more racks, by pulling three suits out, handing them to me, and saying, "Here, any one of these will look great." And she's right.

Now she has a break between patients, so she calls to check in, "I tried the house but you weren't there. What happened? I thought you were supposed to come home today."

I explain the delay and listen to the silence that tells me she's worried and looking for a comforting response. Finally, she says, "I'm sorry, Lil, but it's better that they're being careful, isn't it?"

"Don't try to convince me or humor me," I say petulantly, "I'm depressed and I want to stay that way."

"Oookay," she laughs, dragging out the *o* in her signature way, "be miserable, but talk to me anyway."

We talk for a while and she amuses me with some of her "kid stories"—little-kids-say-the-damndest-things vignettes gleaned from her practice as a child psychologist. By the time we hang up, our laughter has lightened my mood. Her ability to do this, to step back from the moment and find humor, even in some very tough times in her own life, is one of her many gifts. And it's one of the things I love best about our friendship. No matter how hard things may get—and we've shared many very hard times—we always find a way to laugh together. "Thanks," I say as we prepare to say good-bye, "you managed to chase the depression a bit."

"Yeah," she replies, "but I know I can trust you to find it again as soon as I'm gone."

She's not wrong. Left to myself, my mood sinks again. I feel cranky, out of sorts, and tired—tired of being in the hospital, tired of my thoughts, tired of myself. I get out of bed and, pushing my IV stand along, walk up and down the corridors for a while. I feel like the man in my mother's nursing home who pushed his wheel-chair back and forth to nowhere all day long. I read recently that half of all women over sixty-five and a third of all men can expect to spend some of their remaining time in a nursing home. "No," a voice inside me screams, "that's not what's ahead for me; I'll make sure I die first."

From time to time as we've circled around old age, Hank and I have talked about, worried about, and planned for what's ahead. We've agreed that each of us has the right to decide when it's time, as a friend puts it so expressively, "to turn the lights out." And we've given each other our promise to honor the decision and to help implement it when the time comes. If one of us is no longer able, either physically or mentally, to make the choice to die, the other is pledged to take over the task. In case Hank is already gone, or if it's too hard emotionally for him to fulfill the promise, I have a backup, a very old close friend who has agreed to help when and if I call upon her to do so.

I know, of course, that it's easy to make such decisions in the abstract, when the reality is still in the future. I worry about that sometimes. Will I really be able to flip the switch (Why is it so hard to write the words *commit suicide*?) when the time is right? Or will I be tempted to wait just a little bit longer—another day, another week, another month—until I've lost the capacity to decide? I can't know the answer to those questions now; I can know only the resolve I feel today not to allow myself to descend into the helplessness that will rob me of my dignity and humanity.

I'm tired of dragging my IV stand up and down the halls, so I climb back in bed and stare at the ceiling. I hate these feelings, hate whining about my lot, hate myself when I do it. I realize that I dozed off only when I wake with the memory of a dream that's already fading away.

I have a fully dressed newborn infant in my arms, but I have no idea where she came from or why she's dressed in such heavy clothes. I don't know how I know the baby is a girl, since she came to me already clothed, but somehow I'm sure. She squirms around, clearly uncomfortable in the clothes she's wearing. I know I should undress her and get rid of the clothes, but I can't make myself do it, so for a long time I just try to soothe her. After a while she grows so heavy in my arms that I can't hold her, and I put her down and try to undress her. Only now I can't figure out how to do it. No matter how I maneuver, I can't get the clothes off.

A new baby, a new life. *My* life—fully lived, fully clothed like a second skin. The dream tells me I have to take the clothes off, but in the dream, as in life, I resist. I like the life I have, and I know without looking that whatever lies below is inevitably less, not more. So I have no wish to uncover what lies beneath the clothes, let alone to embrace it. Yet I know I have no choice. The clothes I'm wearing are outdated and too heavy for the season that's upon me. I already have the beginnings of a new life; I just don't know yet how to live it.

The only way I know to get rid of the uncomfortable feelings that claim me now is to go into action, so I reach for my computer, check my E-mail, and spend the next hour or so answering the letters that have come in since I logged on last night. That done, I open up the file containing the last chapter of *The Transcendent Child*. I've actually made progress on it and, although I have a way to go, the end is in sight.

My task in this chapter is to sort out the common themes in the life stories I've told and to pull them together into a unified statement about what enables some children to grow into highly functional adults, despite sometimes horrendous childhood stories, while their siblings fall by the wayside. But as I turn to this work I love, work that compensates me so well both emotionally and financially, I'm distracted by images of my mother's work life—the cold, dreary factory where she labored for so long, its windows blackened with an accumulation of years of filth, its walls sweating from the collision of the cold and the steam from the pressing machines, the unending roar of electric-powered machines, the boring, repetitive tasks that took up her day.

My mother's first job was in a factory in Long Island City, a sweatshop where she sewed the linings for the women's coats that were made there. The trip from the Bronx to Long Island City in those days was long and hard. Even today it probably takes over an hour and requires a couple of long subway rides. Then, before some of the lines that are now in service existed, it was a torturous commute that, depending on subway and bus connections, took anywhere from one and a half to two hours.

Each morning she awakened us at five so we could have breakfast before she left. We protested, promising we'd eat if only she'd let us sleep a little later. But this was, for her, an important measure of what a good mother does, so she would never relinquish it. My stomach still curls in revulsion at the sight of oatmeal because it's so linked in my mind with those mornings when I sat there trying to stay awake and gagging as she forced me to eat the lumpy mess in the bowl before me.

As far back as I can remember food was a battleground between me and my mother, a war over power and control. But the fact that it centered on eating wasn't irrelevant—not then, not now. Then, if it wasn't cereal, it was vegetables, which meant overcooked carrots and gray canned peas or string beans. In earlier years, when I was about three and refused to eat, she would force the food down my throat by grabbing my jaw with thumb and middle finger, pressing hard until the pain forced me to open my mouth, and shoving the food in while she held my nose until I either choked or swallowed. When the plate was empty, she turned away with a satisfied, "There, that'll teach you." But what it taught me was unclear. I soon learned to vomit when I wanted to and simply vomited up the food, sometimes all over the table. By the time I was seven and we fought over lumpy oatmeal, that game had stopped. Instead, she stood over me ready to slap me up-side the head until I took a bite and swallowed it.

When I look back over those contests, I wonder how it is that I didn't end up with a serious eating disorder. Not that I got off scot-free. Although the word *bulimia* hadn't yet been coined when I was an adolescent, from the time I was twelve years old I was vomiting up my meals if I decided I'd eaten too much. On those few occasions when my mother caught me, she screamed and hol-lered and threatened mayhem, but by then she knew she had lost the war. I was largely out of her control. Saturday was my fast day when I refused to eat any real food. But in my characteristic way, I wouldn't deprive myself completely. The day was reserved for a chocolate sundae, which I could allow myself to eat only if I'd eaten nothing else all day.

Even today I'm not free of anorexic-like anxieties. When I lis-ten to anorexics talk about what one patient calls her "mind chat-ter" about food, it's very familiar to me. The voices in my head about what I eat and how it will affect my weight—which means how I feel about myself—are rarely silent. And when anyone uses the words *small* or *thin* or *slim* to describe me, I'm always a little surprised. For years I was so convinced I wasn't thin enough to be a size eight that I bought clothes at least one size too big. The difference between me and the seriously eating disordered is that I not only love and appreciate food, I don't deprive myself of its pleasures. But it's never with the unalloyed joy and fulfillment I see in normal people, like my husband. For me, there's always the cal-culus about what it will cost, the promise to "pay it back" tomor-row, and the voice of regret afterward.

Clearly the cultural mandates about the ideal female body, what Kim Chernin has called "the tyranny of slenderness," played a part—still do—in my preoccupation with eating and weight. As does my childhood determination that I'd never look like my mother, with her thick, peasant body. But, as Kim argues so com-pellingly in *The Obsession,* it isn't the body alone—not just its size and shape, the firmness of the thighs, the roundness of the breasts, the flatness of the belly, the sleek boyishness of the hips—that underlies women's eating disorders. Beneath the fetish about the body and its weight is a deeper, more serious concern about the expression of the self in all its fullness, about the acceptability of our natural passions and "appetites," about where they will lead us if given free rein. It was just those passions, the appetite for living and feeling more fully, that I fought so hard for in my mother's house. I won the war but its lessons were driven into my soul. Not just about food, but *especially* about food. Then, each victory exacted a cost. Now, each meal that seems like an indulgence demands repayment.

Having done her duty by feeding us, my mother rushed off to work and my brother went back to bed. I could never get to sleep again. When I was little, those early-morning hours when it was still dark outside were frighteningly lonely. Later, when books became my companions, the quiet hours before I had to leave for school felt more friendly, a time when I could think my own thoughts and read without interruption.

When my mother arrived at work, she took her place among the dozens of women who sat hunched over their sewing machines in a large, noisy, dank, and airless room. Eight hours a day on Monday through Friday and four on Saturday they sat there, their hands and feet flying, an occasional shrill scream punctuating the air when, in their haste, they didn't get a thumb or forefinger out of the way of the machine's needle. They were pieceworkers, these women, paid a few cents for every garment they sewed. No benefits, no overtime, just the privilege of working long hours in abominable conditions for subsistence wages.

I never saw the factory in Long Island City, but I saw several others when, later, my mother found work in Manhattan. They were always the same—the same dirt, the same noise, the same lint-clogged air, the same foul smell, the same cold in the winter, the same oppressive heat in the summer, and the same row upon row of women doing the same repetitive task, hour after hour, day after day, year after year.

For pieceworkers speed is essential if they're to make enough money to feed their families. And my mother soon boasted that she was the fastest worker in the group. But with wages so low, it didn't make much difference. No matter how many hours she worked, no matter how fast she pushed herself and her machine, she earned barely enough to make ends meet, even with the most careful budgeting.

For most people, the social relations on the job—the comradeship, the quick exchange in the hall, the gossip in the bathroom or at the water cooler—provide one of the reasons for getting up and going to work every day. But for pieceworkers, as my mother used to say, "Time is money"—a reality that made it hard for any kind of real companionship to flourish at work. There were brief moments of friendly banter before the workday began. But even if the management had allowed talk among the workers, even if the nearly deafening noise of fifty or a hundred machines hadn't inhibited it, the women couldn't afford it. Once they slid behind their machines and the power was turned on, every minute spent in conversation meant a smaller paycheck at the end of the week. Even bathroom breaks were taken only in extreme need—so extreme that many times my mother would rush to the bathroom as she came through the front door at night, there to heave an enormous sigh of relief as she finally let go of the urine stream she had held in for so many hours.

When I was older, maybe nine or ten, and my mother was working in Manhattan, I'd occasionally meet her at the factory at the end of her day, usually as part of some special treat like a meal at the automat, a New York institution of the era where the food was displayed in little windowed cubicles that opened magically to deliver up your sandwich when you put a nickel or two in the slot. These were exciting events—going downtown on the subway by myself, anticipating our outing, planning ways to assure that my mother would be in good humor.

Each time I entered the factory to wait for my mother, I was assailed by a mixture of fascination and repulsion. I'd stand in a corner waiting for the bell to signal that the power to the machines was about to be turned off and the workday was over, and I'd think, "I'll never work here." I hated the look, feel, smell, and noise of the place. I hated the women in the office who treated the factory workers with such disdain—women who themselves were no more than a few years away from the factory yet who, when they had to come onto the factory floor, sniffed and picked their way through, holding their skirts tightly to their sides so as not to be sullied by contact with anything or anyone there.

But I was also impressed by the economy of motion as I watched my mother's hands fly through her tasks, her head bowed, her concentration intense. It was a primitive kind of production line, but it worked. On the floor to my mother's left sat a pile of linings that were already sewn at the shoulders; on her right were those she had finished. My mother's job was to sew the side seams. Without lifting her head or breaking her rhythm, she took a lining from the pile on her left, sewed the seams, and in a swift, perfectly synchronized motion, dropped it on the floor to her right at the same time as reached for the next one on her left. Every now and then, a floor woman would come by, leave another batch of half-finished linings, pick up those my mother had worked on, count them, and deliver them to the next stop on the production line— the women who sewed in the sleeves.

Not surprisingly, there was plenty of room for error in the system. Sometimes they were legitimate mistakes. Often they were the result of deliberate undercounts, one of the many ways factory owners found to cheat the workers so they could squeeze out a little extra profit. But in 1931, the year my mother became a garment worker, the International Ladies Garment Workers Union (ILGWU) was still a couple of years away from its first major success in organizing the industry. Until the union became a force to be reckoned with, workers had little recourse; any complaint was likely to get them fired. So they seethed but kept quiet.

For those of us whose lives revolved around the garment industry, there were five seasons of the year instead of the usual four: winter, spring, summer, fall, and the dreaded *slack season*—as real a part of our lives as the winter snow and the summer sun. During the four regular seasons, when fashions changed to match the weather and the mood, factories hummed away as they churned out the clothing that women looked forward to so eagerly. But as each season waned, so did the work, and the workers were sent home to wait for the next season and worry about how their families would make it until then.

In good times a worker could believe that work would come when the new line went into production. But during the Depression, no one knew if the company would survive into the next season. The social programs that later would provide some security in hard times—unemployment insurance, social security, Medicare, Medicaid, and some kind of federal guarantee of aid to poor families—were still only a radical's dream. So we waited and worried in a nightmare of uncertainty.

The anxiety of those times still lives in my bones. My mother looked frantically for other work, but there was rarely any to be found. With her first savings, she bought a sewing machine—one of those old foot-operated machines that people now buy as antiques—and began to do alterations for others. I used to watch her work at that machine with awe—the coordination of her feet and her fingers, the swiftness with which they worked, the rhythmic clack of the machine's treadle that never missed a beat.

Since we had no telephone, an employer could reach my mother to summon her back to work only through a message at the corner candy store. Sometimes when someone called, the owner would send one of his children up to call my mother while the caller hung on at the other end of the line. Often, however, they simply took a message and waited for her to come around and ask about calls. As the weeks went by and she became more and more uneasy, she'd run off to the candy store a half-dozen times a day to ask about messages. Or she'd trek downtown to the factory in the hope of getting some reassuring news.

My mother, one of the world's most frugal women, usually managed to have some savings to help tide us over the slack season, a feat she accomplished by forgoing most small comforts during the months when she was bringing home a paycheck. We still had no radio; we wouldn't see a telephone in our house for years; leaving an electric light on beyond what was absolutely necessary was a crime of high order; even a subway ride, then only a nickel, was taken only when it was impossible to walk.

Occasionally we'd get a penny to spend at the candy store, a big moment that found me standing at the counter for many long minutes while I agonized over what to choose from the array of delectables that teased and tempted me. Once in a while we got a nickel to go to the movies, the favored Saturday afternoon activity for the neighborhood kids. Every now and then she'd bring home an edible treat, usually a whipped cream cake she loved.

But that was it. We had a roof over our heads, she reminded us repeatedly when we asked for something more, and food on the table. As far as she was concerned, nothing else was important. Nothing, that is, except shoes. Other clothing was of no consequence. We would make do with whatever she managed to beg, borrow, or sew. But she worried about our feet, so the one thing we got was new shoes when we needed them.

Why shoes? Because her feet hurt all the time, a problem she attributed to the fact that she never had decent fitting shoes as a child. Like her insistence upon feeding us breakfast at five in the morning, good shoes were the symbol of her ability to care properly for her children, a visible statement not just to the world but to herself that she was a conscientious and caring mother.

During the slack season, the occasional treats disappeared, and meals got skimpier and less interesting—no small accomplishment given how bad they were in normal times. As the weeks of unemployment piled up, we hunkered down into a real subsistence level. Meat, chicken, even fish, which then was one of the cheaper foods, were replaced by vegetables accompanied sometimes by rice or potatoes and an occasional egg or some cottage cheese. But even this stripped-down life usually didn't keep us from running out of money before it was over.

We were saved from disaster by a two-thousand-dollar life insurance policy my father bought a few years before his death. It was common then for such insurance policies to be sold door-to-door, especially in poor immigrant neighborhoods. There, where people knew firsthand about all kinds of hardships and calamities, including early deaths, it wasn't hard for a salesman to convince a man that his family needed the security a life insurance policy offered. The terms were easy—ten or fifteen cents a week. And they didn't even have to go anywhere to pay their money; the salesman came around regularly to collect.

In the years immediately following my father's death, my mother relied on that insurance money to get us through the worst times. She tapped it carefully and only when she had no choice—when she ran out of money for food, when we were threatened with eviction. But even that small cushion would soon be lost in the bank failures of 1932.

For my mother, and for the millions of others whose life savings were swept away with a turn of a key in a lock, the unthinkable happened. Hundreds of banks all over the country simply closed their doors. I don't remember how she heard the news, only that she flew out of the house in a panic and raced the few blocks to the bank, commanding me to stay put as she ran out the door. But I was too frightened by her anguished cries to obey.

I caught up with her just as she reached the bank, where hundreds of others had already congregated. Some were so shocked they could only stand there silently, not believing what they saw. Others were shouting and pounding on the locked doors while the few bank employees who were still inside peeked out helplessly. Like a wild woman, my mother pushed through the crowd and joined those who were demanding entry. I can still see her, her fists beating furiously on the closed doors, her eyes wild with terror, her lips calling down the wrath of God with every Jewish curse and invective at her command.

I stood at the edge of the crowd fearful and bewildered. Something terrible had happened, but I didn't understand what it was. Why were they banging on the doors and windows when it was clear the bank was closed? Why were they weeping and shouting as if someone had died? I tried to reach my mother but couldn't get through the mass of people that grew larger with every passing minute. I wanted to go home, to run from the terror and rage that filled the air. But I was afraid to move, afraid to leave my mother, afraid I'd never see her again if I did.

Finally, the police came and, threatening the crowd with their nightsticks, quickly broke it up. Defeated, my mother turned and walked home slowly, all the while talking as much to herself as to me. How could a bank simply close its doors? This was America; such things didn't happen here. The bank, she had been told, was the one safe place for her money. Now it was gone. What could she ever believe in again? For a woman who already looked so suspiciously at the world, the bank closings confirmed for her that she could trust nothing or no one.

Chapter Twelve

It has been six weeks since I left the hospital and plunged immediately back into my busy daily routines. I see about sixteen patients each week and divide the rest of my time between writing, giving an occasional lecture, and the usual social activities of a life. But my denial mechanisms, normally so efficient, aren't working so well and, no matter how busy I keep myself, I can't escape the sense of fragility and vulnerability with which I now live.

Even my visits to the gym, the one place where I can almost always empty my mind of everything but the muscles necessary to lift the weights, don't always allow for forgetfulness. And in those brief moments when I do forget, my calendar calls me back to reality each time it reminds me to get my pro time test. My doctor assures me that we should be able to stabilize my pro time and stretch out my lab visits soon, but meanwhile the numbers go up and down like a yo-yo, and I'm still being tested weekly.

Perhaps because I've been feeling so vulnerable, I'm more preoccupied than usual with my aging. My friend Dorothy, one of my few close friends who is also my age mate, laughs when I say that. She and I have shared the marker birthdays—those that end in zeros—for nearly four decades, and she now reminds me: "It seems to me you've been concerned about your age since you turned fifty. You've always had more trouble than I do because I didn't have as much to lose; I was never beautiful."

I demur. I've always known I'm attractive; I did a brief stint as a photographer's model in my late teens. But I'm uncomfortable both with the comparison she makes between us and with the knowledge that there's some truth in what she says. "I don't know about that," I say aloud, while inside I'm remembering the many times when my good looks gave me a distinct edge, especially in the job market.

More than once, when I worked as a secretary in my youth, I was hired over a woman whose credentials were as good or better than mine but whose face and figure couldn't compete. Thinking about how my looks have advantaged me at various times in my life makes me feel uneasy and sets me to wondering: Will I ever get over feeling uncomfortable about such privilege? I know this is guilt speaking, the guilt of being the transcendent child, the one who got out when my brother couldn't. But that doesn't stop me from wanting to shout, "Hey, wait a minute; it's not my fault. I didn't ask for those privileges; it's the way of the world we live in." But I also remember how often I was glad to have them, and I know I don't like seeing those advantages slip away into old age. And why should I? It's another of the insults of aging in a society that reveres youth and beauty above all else.

While these thoughts are roaming around in my mind, a young colleague who's writing a book about women in their middle years calls wanting to talk about her work. "It's depressing to see how much hasn't changed since you wrote *Women of a Certain Age*," she says, referring to my book published in 1979. "We fought so hard to be taken seriously; we didn't want to be judged by our looks. We grew hair under our arms and didn't shave our legs, and we hated it when guys whistled at us on the street. Now when we go by a construction site and no one whistles, we feel a pang of regret and complain that we're invisible."

I hear this story from women all the time, women who were accustomed to being noticed and as "good" feminists sometimes resented it, now feel the sting of being unseen. Just recently Diane, a very attractive fifty-year-old, commented ruefully about how she has begun to feel invisible at times. "I was standing in line at the checkout counter and there was this cute guy at the cash register who was flirting like mad with the thirty-year-old behind me. I couldn't believe it. I was always the one guys noticed and flirted with, and he never even saw me. I just stood there thinking, 'Hey, what about me?' "

Whether fifty or eighty, the story is the same. Mary Cantwell, writing in the *New York Times* about an interview with the novelist Jean Rhys, then in her eighties, tells Rhys, "You know what I miss as I get older? That look of anticipation in a man's eyes when he first meets you." Rhys responds with a sigh, "Yes, I miss it still."

Once in a while the chagrin of not being seen is soothed by the exhilarating moment when we are, as I found out recently on a beautiful Sunday afternoon that was rendered even more wonderful by the unexpected attention. My husband and I had been browsing at a street fair, wandering among the booths and making noises about the terrible art on display when we came upon a booth selling straw hats. We laughed as I tried on one silly hat after another until I found one that worked. "I like that, buy it," he urged. It didn't exactly go with my too-big T-shirt, my jeans, and the sweater tied around my waist, but it was rakish, so I wore it anyway.

After walking wherever our feet took us for several hours, we found ourselves on the edge of North Beach, tired and wanting to go home. While my husband stood ten or fifteen feet away waving at passing cabs, I leaned against the lamppost on the corner relishing the last of a lovely day, regretting that it would soon come to an end. A few minutes later a man, scrubbed, well dressed, probably in his late forties or early fifties, came by, and while he waited for the light to change, smiled and said, "Hey, howya doin'?"

"Fine," I answered with a smile. "It's a gorgeous day, isn't it."

"Yeah, sure is," he said. Then he leaned toward me, lowered his voice, and with a wide smile asked, "Say, mama, you hustlin'? 'Cause if you're sellin', I'm buyin'."

I was so taken aback that it took a few seconds before I understood what he was asking. When I finally got it, I burst out laughing and wanted to hug him. To be seen as a desirable woman at my age, even one who was "sellin'," was a gift, not an affront.

Hank and I laughed about the incident all the way home, but I found myself reflecting on my response to it for several days afterward. As an ardent feminist I knew I should be offended. But as an aging woman who feels the loss of her public sexual presence, I was reminded once again that we can force our minds and mouths to hew to the politically correct line, but our emotions aren't so easily boxed in.

I smile now when I recall the incident, as I do whenever it comes to mind. And I feel sympathy for the younger women who are now beginning to suffer the slights of invisibility—the baby boomers for whom growing old was once unthinkable, who refused to bow to conventional definitions of beauty when their youth alone made them desirable, and who now must face the loss of it.

I'm reminded, too, of my own angst as each of those birthdays that marked off a decade approached. I don't mean that I sat around thinking grand thoughts about life and its meaning. But my heart would grow inexplicably heavy from time to time, and periodically I'd find myself filled with a sense of dread.

In some ways fifty may have been the worst because it was such a powerful confrontation between external reality and internal illusion. Fifty made no sense in my internal life; I didn't feel any different from when I was twenty or thirty. A sensibility that was reinforced by the fact that, having come very late to my career (I became a freshman at Berkeley at thirty-nine and was awarded my doctorate eight years later, at forty-seven), I was just at the beginning of the life that would engage me for the next few decades. My peers were not the fifty-year-old men who had been my professors, but the twenty-five-year-old students with whom I shared the challenges and triumphs of graduate school. I couldn't be fifty; I felt too young to be so old. A week before the big day, I allowed a friend to talk me into dyeing my hair, which had turned gray in my twenties. I figured at fifty no one would ever again comment on the starkness of that gray hair on a young face.

Sixty was easier; perhaps because I'd survived fifty, because all my anticipatory angst seemed so ridiculous when the day finally came and nothing changed. I didn't suddenly turn into a bitter, angry replica of my mother. I was no different the day after I turned fifty than I had been the day before—no different inside, that is. Outside I had become a honey-colored blonde. At sixty even that remained the same.

"Wait until sixty-five; there's no avoiding that one," I told myself. At sixty-five your age, which until then had been a strictly private affair, becomes a public one. That's when the federal government drops a Medicare card on your desk; when airlines, buses, subways, and movie theaters offer senior discounts; when your local food market probably promises a discount on your purchases—provided, that is, that you shop at the time that's convenient for them. The assumption being that you have nothing better to do than to conform to their needs.

Despite the public notice that made sixty-five loom so large for me, that birthday tiptoed in more like a brief April shower than the heavy winter storm I'd anticipated. I put my Medicare card in my wallet and refused to step up to claim my senior discounts wherever I went. Since neither the years nor my physical appearance matched the self that lived inside me, I saw no reason to acknowledge my age in those places. I laugh now at the ridiculous places in which I chose to protest and hide from the reality. For in fact, I had no problem talking easily about my age on a lecture platform, probably because I knew it would always bring a gasp of disbelief from the audience. But somehow I couldn't make myself advertise it at the ticket booth of the movie theater or the counter of the supermarket.

Seventy was another story. That, as we Californians say as we wait for the earth to shake us up perhaps one last time, was *the big one.* How did I live long enough to get so old? From the time I had my initial bout of thrombophlebitis after my first daughter was born (the one who died soon after), I never expected to live this long. When, contrary to my doctors' orders, Marci was born a year and a half later and I got sick again, I only hoped I would live long enough to raise her to adulthood. Suddenly I was seventy with no sign of giving it up any time soon.

I'd look at myself sometimes and think: "What's the big deal;

you're no different than you were before you turned seventy." Only it was the outside that was no different. Inside I knew I'd stepped over a line and there was no going back to my former denial. If I still couldn't quite tell myself I was old, at least I knew I was only one small step away from it.

I still worked out at the gym, still walked up and down the steep hills and two miles that separate my home and office, still flew back and forth across the country in two or three days to fulfill a lecture commitment, still kept the hectic pace of my life before seventy. Only now I knew that both my body and my brain did better if I gave them a little more rest. My muscles told me that they needed several days between visits to the gym to perform as I wanted them to; my brain insisted it could no longer work late into the night. None of this happened overnight, of course; it clearly had been happening for some years. But it wasn't until my seventieth birthday that I could listen to the messages my body was sending. Which may say as much about the psychological aspects of aging as the physical ones.

Seventy-three should have been a nonevent, but my mother just died; I've suffered a near-death experience, and my husband is about to turn eighty. Until now I lived my life heedless of my own mortality. Call it stupidity, call it denial, call it willed unconsciousness—however we label it, it remains the truth. Having looked death in the face, however, I find myself asking questions I've never asked before. Just a few weeks ago my thoughts, when I went for a walk, would most likely turn to today's problems—how to frame a chapter in the book I'm working on; how to resolve some stuck place with a patient. Now, as I wander through my beloved city, I'm fretting about tomorrow—about how I want to live what I now know is the concluding chapter of my life. In the past my concerns about aging centered on whether my health and sanity would allow me to live my old age well, which meant that I could keep doing what I was doing. Now I'm trying to figure out how I *want* to live these years, not knowing anymore whether the life I've lived until now is the one I want to take me into the future.

In the weeks since I've been home, I finished *The Transcendent*

Child and sent it off to my publisher, where it will be pummeled and pampered into its final shape and delivered into the world nine months from now—the same gestation period as for a child. Every book is a learning experience for its author, not just about the subject matter but about one's self. And each one takes its own toll in the writing. This one, with its life histories of eight women and men who managed, as an old Buddhist saying goes, to fall down seven times and get up eight, was so close to my heart, so much a part of my own life and concerns, that it brought a kind of pain and pleasure I hadn't known before.

I have no plans for writing anything else right now. In my past life . . . Startling words; I had no idea I was thinking them until I saw them on the page. What do they mean? If the life I've known is past, what's ahead? More important: Do I really have to give up the past before I can move into the future? I've done that twice before—the first time when my first husband and I moved from New York to Los Angeles nearly fifty years ago; the second when I left that marriage ten years later, married Hank a couple of years after that, and moved with him to the San Francisco Bay Area. But each of those times I was leaving a life I wanted to put behind me, while the years since have been fulfilling, rewarding, productive, and happy beyond any dreams I might ever have had.

I don't mean that I wanted to forget the life (*lives*, really, since each seems so discrete, as if lived by someone else) I lived before Hank, although for a long time I managed to do just that with much of my childhood. But whatever the issues between my ex-husband and me, whatever the angers and hurts we visited upon each other, I've always felt grateful for those years. For one thing, they gave me my daughter; that alone would be reason enough for gratitude. But they were important personal years as well, providing me with a safer harbor than any I'd ever known—a relatively protected place within which I could grow from the child who married at nineteen-going-on-twelve to the thirty-six-year-old woman I had become by the time I left.

So what was I thinking when I wrote the words "in my past life"? Perhaps I attribute too much to a slip of the fingers. It's an occupational hazard. I was trying to say simply that if I were still doing what I've always done, I would already have moved on to the work on midlife families—analyzing my data, looking for the patterns of behavior and feeling that made the interviews so interesting, and getting ready to begin the book for which I have a contract. Now the interviews sit accusingly on a shelf just above my computer while I dawdle with other things.

I keep telling myself that I should get to work and try to rekindle my interest in the study by rereading a few interviews or having a conversation with a colleague about some of my findings. But something inside stops me short of sitting down to the serious work of beginning a book. And I worry, "Have I lost touch with the place inside me from which my writing has come?"

Diane and I have dinner to talk about what has now become in my mind THE BOOK. She has been close to my work for more than two decades, is one of my toughest critics, and since she has recently turned fifty herself, she qualifies as one of the midlife people I've been studying. As always, she has plenty of ideas, and we spend hours turning them this way and that, pushing the edge of the intellectual envelope, each of us stimulated by the other's thoughts.

I go home exhilarated and feel ready to get to work. "I'm lucky to have such friends in my life," I think as I prepare for bed. Each friendship is unique, of course, each relationship differently nuanced. But all of them, the women and the men, share in common the qualities of warmth, loyalty, a sense of humor, and the kind of intelligence and breadth of mind that never fail to interest me. I don't mean that the people I call my friends are perfect, any more than I am, or that these relationships are free of conflict and ambivalence. I know there are things about me each of these friends would change if they could (they frequently tell me so), just as there are qualities I wish I could change in them. But none of that impinges on the love and respect we have for each other.

I awaken early the next morning and go eagerly to my computer. But the spark I felt last night is gone, and I'm left with nothing but a blank screen. I sit there worrying about the loss of my creative energy, fearful that some force in me that has given direction to my life may have died. Or maybe it's more mundane than that; maybe, after nine books, I've just run out of anything interesting to say.

For weeks I torture myself with questions, probing my internal life ceaselessly as I try to understand what's happening to me. How can it be that this thing that has been at the center of my life for so long no longer engages me? But the one thing I can't listen to easily is the voice inside me that says simply, I don't want to.

I don't want to! What do those words mean? I have never not wanted to write. They must be a screen for something more, something deeper that I don't yet understand. But what if there's nothing more complicated than that; what if I really don't want to? It's a nearly unthinkable thought. Without my work I'm lost. If I don't write this book, what will I do? More worrisome: If I'm not writing, who am I? Will I turn into a dull and uninteresting old woman? After all my struggle, will my end be no different than my mother's?

Sometime during these agonizing days my friend Barry phones from Los Angeles. We speak regularly, once every week or so, but this time it seems to me that our conversation is uncharacteristically desultory. "Was it my fault?" I worry when we hang up. "Will he begin to think I'm boring if I don't have anything more interesting to say?"

If I'm not investing my usual drive and energy in my work, what will take its place? I tell myself it's all right just to enjoy the sunshine, to plan a weekend away, to go to New York for a few days for no reason other than to see a couple of plays and visit some friends. But is this a LIFE?

What do people do in their old age? Surely there's a way to live these years productively and still have time to, as they say, "watch the flowers grow." I used to be one of those people who never really understood what those words meant. Now when I think I should be working instead of walking down by the bay and drinking in the beauty of the fog as it rolls over the bridge and the hills of Marin, I'm mindful of the caution that no one ever lay on her deathbed regretting the fact that she didn't work more. But knowing that doesn't answer my question about how to live a life without a serious engagement with work.

Hank's birthday is coming closer, and we've begun to talk about what he'd like to do in celebration. *Celebration!* I feel as if I'm being invited to a funeral and he wants to celebrate. Although he hasn't said so, I know he'd like a party, an event where he would be surrounded with friends and family with whom he could share both his feelings for them and his love of life. But I don't think I can do it. I know I'm being selfish, that instead of considering him I'm thinking only about myself, but something inside me keeps screaming, "I can't."

We talk about it often as we go for a walk or sit over a table at one of our favorite restaurants in the city. But no matter how hard I try, there's no place inside me that understands why he wants to celebrate turning eighty. I get the words but the music eludes me. I hear it when he tells me that turning eighty, especially in the way he's about to do it, has particular meaning because of his own difficult relationship with his autocratic father, who was senile at eighty and died two years later. My head grasps that, for Hank, a healthy, happy, young-looking eighty is an achievement, a triumph over a father who could never let anyone else win, and a relief from the fear that his father's old age would also be his own.

But no explanation, no intellectual understanding, makes me any easier about this milestone (minefield?) we're approaching. I can't bear to think that I might lose him, can't bear the knowledge that our time together is so limited. Yet not a day goes by when I don't conjure with that reality. I talk with a friend about a plan for next year—a symphony or theater series, a vacation—as if I know it will happen. But inside a voice says, "*If* there's a next year." I haven't figured out yet how to live with such a time-limited view.

My thoughts about my husband's aging and death engender feelings that are very old at the same time that they leave me feeling very young, a remnant, no doubt, of the anguish and loss I suffered in the aftermath of my father's death. But I ask myself also whether my angst about him is a displacement from my own unacknowledged fears about myself. Hard as it is, it may be easier for me to count up the signs of slippage in him than in me.

In fact, although he's nearly eight years older than I am, he has no sign of the kind of serious illness that has recently befallen me. And his days are anything but quiet and sedentary. He has written about food and wine for years and continues to do so. Now, as he approaches his eightieth birthday his first book, a memoir about his experiences in the Lincoln Brigades during the Spanish Civil War, has been accepted for publication, and he already has a second near completion, this one an encyclopedia of knowledge about food and cooking. All this while teaching three days a week and spreading his artistic wings in the glass fusion work he loves.

I watch my husband with a hyper-vigilance that's disconcerting to both of us. I try to fool myself sometimes into thinking that I can hide my anxiety well enough to escape his notice, but in truth he'd have to be comatose to miss it. Sometimes we laugh about how alert I am to any sign of his aging, no matter how small—a slip in memory, a wrong turn on a familiar route, some breathlessness when we climb the steep hill outside our front door, a nap taken more often than usual. At other times it becomes so oppressive that he protests, "I've always loved your attention, but maybe we could have a little less of it right now."

I understand how he feels; I would hate it if he did this to me. So I try to back off, to go about my own life without focusing so closely on his. "It will be better after this birthday," I tell myself. And it is.

The dilemma of how to celebrate eighty is resolved when we decide on a long weekend in Santa Fe, New Mexico, with Marci and Larry. He likes the idea because we don't often get to spend that much uninterrupted time with them. Meanwhile, unknown to him, I've arranged to have Blake, our grandson, and several of our closest friends from various parts of the country—sixteen in all—join us in Santa Fe for a surprise dinner. Marci takes over the logistics of hotel reservations and arrival times and I make the dinner arrangements. By now he's so convinced that my angst about eighty won't allow for anything more than the quiet weekend we've planned that he suspects nothing until he walks into the room and is greeted by a sea of loving faces before him. It's a moment no one who was there will ever forget.

Chapter Thirteen

It's raining, a violent winter storm that darkens the morning sky and sends sheets of water lashing against my windows. The radio reports traffic accidents, pileups, and endless delays, especially on the bridges that take commuters in and out of the city—a perfect day to stimulate the road rage we've been hearing so much about recently.

I have a meeting at the university in Berkeley today and I'm trying to decide whether I really have to go. It's too sloppy outside to walk the mile downhill to BART, and the Bay Bridge, which separates San Francisco from Berkeley, is a mess. I stand by the wall of windows in my study looking at the gray heaviness on the western horizon, a sign that this storm is here for a while. After a few minutes, conscience and duty assert themselves, and I gather myself together and head to the garage for my car.

All the approaches to the bridge are jammed, so I sit in a long line of cars that crawls forward a few feet at time. My car is totally boxed in, unable to move forward or backward, so I have no choice but to wait. Impatient, some drivers keep up a steady din with their horns, others climb out of their cars and defy the rain in the hope that they can see what's delaying us. I turn the music up and try to shut out my own impatience when my attention is caught by two men who seem to be arguing about something. Suddenly one jumps into his car, sets it in motion, and rams into the car of the other.

I know I'm perfectly safe in my own car, but I feel unaccountably frightened at this reminder of the damage that such uncontrolled rage can do. Where does it come from? I ask for maybe the thousandth time, as memories of my mother's inexplicable rages wash over me. My mind sees her screaming at me with hate-filled eyes; my body feels the hurt as the flat of her hand whips across my face; my heart feels the humiliation and degradation of her assault; my soul fills with anger and hate.

I used to wonder sometimes who or what started it all. Did I make the distance between us, or did she? Now I know that these are useless questions; we both did our part. I didn't submit easily to her rageful authoritarianism; she never gave up the struggle to impose her will. For my mother, whose life must often have seemed so out of control, I'm sure she felt it imperative to stay in command of her children. For me, asserting my independence, whether in thought or action, felt like a struggle for my life, the only way I could resist being crushed by her.

As an adult I can feel sympathy for her—sympathy, and even something like admiration, for the courage she displayed in the face of the obstacles life put in her path, for the stubborn determination that made it possible to keep her children and make a home for us. But she also made our lives a lot harder than they had to be. For her anger and inability to trust others not only made her children miserable but quickly put her on a collision course with anyone who came close. And once down that road, there was no turning back.

In my own case, it wasn't unusual for her to banish me, to treat me as if I didn't exist, usually because I'd committed some minor crime, sometimes for no reason I could fathom. True, she couldn't put me out of her life forever as she did others. But she could and did stop talking to me, sometimes for two weeks at a time, a punishment that was much worse than any physical abuse she ever inflicted. No matter what I did, how good I tried to be, how many peace overtures I made, how long and pitifully I cried, nothing moved her until she decided I'd had enough.

The days during these periods were terrible. But it's the nights

I remember most vividly because, from the time my father died until I was nineteen, my mother and I shared a bed. After enduring her steely silence by day, I would lie in bed at night feeling the heat of her body next to mine, one part of me wanting to crawl back inside her and another wanting to get as far away as I could from her flesh, which was so soft yet so unyielding. When she'd roll up against me during the night, I'd wake feeling frightened, as if her touch was somehow dangerous. To this day, I don't like being touched when I'm sleeping. I treasure my husband's embraces when I'm awake, but once the lights go out and we're ready for sleep, I withdraw to the far end of our king-size bed and keep a no-man's land between us through the night.

Even though I felt mistreated, rejected, and angry, I lived in terror that my mother would die or disappear again. She was, after all, the only parent I had. So in those early years, each evening would find me standing at the subway station (which in the Bronx, where we lived, was an elevated line) waiting anxiously for her to come home from work. As each train arrived with no sign of her, I became more and more agitated. What if something happened to her? What would my brother and I do? Where would we go? If they sent us to an orphanage, would we be able to stay together? We weren't close, he and I, but if she disappeared, he was all I had.

I was seven or eight, old enough to know that she wouldn't be happy to see me waiting at the foot of the station's steps. Yet the relief when I saw her made up for the angry words with which she so often greeted me: "Why are you standing there like an orphan?" Even when she didn't react angrily, there was never a smile when she caught sight of me, never a glimmer of empathy or understanding of the fear that brought me there. Yet so powerful were the feelings driving me that I was impelled to play out the same scenario night after night for a long time.

I wonder now if her anger was a way of warding off her helplessness in the face of her child's fear. Or perhaps my anxieties mirrored her own so strongly that she had to shut out all awareness lest it debilitate her. I'll never know because she rarely was open to any discussion of the past, assuming before a word was spoken that it was founded in blame and ill will. Long after we were adults, she still had only two responses when either my brother or I tried to share a memory or understand an event from our childhood. The first and most likely was "It never happened." Failing that, she would burst into a defensive recitation of the hardships she had endured; repeat the line we'd heard a thousand times: "Other mothers would have sent their children to an orphanage" and complain because we didn't appreciate her sacrifices.

Sacrifice! It's the ultimate mother word. In a society that holds a woman wholly responsible for the care of her children, that blames her when they don't turn out just right, women often ward off guilt about their maternal imperfections, real or imagined, by reminding themselves and others of the sacrifices they made. Was this partly what motivated my mother's frequent references to her sacrifices?

The question evokes a complicated response in me—part child, part adult. The child says sullenly, "Yeah, well who asked for your sacrifices? Maybe you should have sacrificed less and loved us more." But the adult wonders if, somewhere inside, she understood that she wasn't a very good mother, certainly not the mother her children needed—knowledge that would have been intolerable without her claim to sacrifice.

At the same time that I lived in fear of losing my mother, by the time I was seven years old I also began to *dis*identify with her and to remove myself psychologically from the family scene. I don't mean that I didn't need her, didn't long for her approval, or even that I didn't love her as a child loves a parent. The rare hug, the smile I saw so seldom, the few times she walked by and dropped a gentle hand on my head—these stand out in memory as moments of pure pleasure, moments when my love for her swelled my heart. But it was love tempered by a confused and contradictory set of feelings—by my hurt and bewilderment in the face of her rage and rejection, by moments of passionate hatred, by the knowledge, in whatever way a seven-year-old knows, that I didn't want to model myself on this person who was so mean and angry.

Whatever the success of my efforts to disidentify with my mother, it's also true that I was like her in some ways, not least in the kind of determination I was capable of when I made up my mind to do something. It's a lasting gift, one that's an important contributor to whatever success I've had in my adult life. Paradoxically, it's the same legacy that marks my identification with her that also made it possible to disidentify, to dream of other ways of being, of another kind of life, even when I didn't yet have any idea what that life might look like.

All I knew then was that I met any suggestion that I might be like my mother with a stubborn resolve to change. When I was about eight years old a girl who lived in my building watched me walk down the street and remarked as I approached her, "You walk just like your mother."

"I do not," I retorted, and fled feeling shamed and angry. But I couldn't run from her words.

Back in our apartment, I climbed up on a chair in front of the bathroom mirror to see whether what she said was true, but I couldn't see my feet. I ran outside and around the corner, where I could see my reflection in the store windows, and checked my walk from every angle. When my mother came home that night, I watched her carefully and saw, to my dismay, that my neighbor was right.

I spent the next year training myself to walk differently. Sixty-five years later I still monitor my walk from time to time, experiencing the same satisfaction I knew then when I no longer walked like her. A symbolic gesture, perhaps, but no less important in my struggle to prove to myself that I was different than when I became an assimilated American girl who spoke English only, who read books, who worked so hard at being thin when she was thick. My success in each of these was more than symbolism; together all those victories showed me what was possible when I made up my mind to do something.

Outwardly I remained part of the family. I lived in the house, did what was expected, tried earnestly from time to time to relate to my brother, to please my mother—rarely with any success. Inwardly I found more and more ways to separate myself from them, both in the real world and in my imaginary one.

To comfort me in my internal world, I decided I must be an adopted child and fantasized that in some heroic, romantic quest I would find my true family, the one in which I would finally belong. That didn't happen, of course, because this *was* my true family, the family of my birth. But it didn't stop me from inventing a family complete with a father, a loving stay-at-home mom who cooked cereal without lumps, a sister who was my emotional twin, a big brother who liked to play with me, and, not least, a bed of my own. A fantasy family that sometimes felt more real than the one I lived with every day.

Outside the house, the treasures of New York City beckoned to me. Although my home was a cultural wasteland, I was fortunate to grow up at a time when the city's school system was still intact and when its marvelous museums were open to the public free of charge. It was at school that I first heard a piece of classical music and sat enthralled by the sound. There, too, I was exposed to the wonders of the Metropolitan Museum of Art, to which my class was taken on a field trip. Later, as a teenager, I would go there to look at the paintings, hungering to be in the presence of beauty I couldn't fully understand.

These experiences not only put me in touch with a world I might never have known otherwise, they also showed me new ways of differentiating myself from my family. If they didn't read books, I would gobble them up. If they had no interest in going to an art museum, I would become a steady visitor. If they liked only popular tunes, I would listen to classical music.

It's true that these activities isolated me from them still further. They resented what my mother called my "highfalutin ideas"; I felt contemptuous of their ignorance. But my ability to escape into another world also contributed to a heightened sense of efficacy and a more autonomous sense of self. For difficult as it was to feel like an alien in my family, it was my ability to accept my marginality, to acknowledge that I didn't fit, that laid the psychological foundation that enabled me to see and grasp alternatives when they came into view.

This was the crucial difference between my brother and me. He couldn't see beyond the walls my mother erected. No matter how hard she made life at home, she was also his savior, the parent who didn't die and leave him—a perception that locked them into a hostile embrace that helped to ruin his life.

When, in later years, my mother would occasionally speak of my childhood, she would acknowledge that I never gave her "any trouble," which meant she didn't have to worry about my grades in school or about my getting into scrapes on the street. But she'd also follow this somewhat grudging concession by complaining, "You were always peculiar, not like your brother."

Chapter Fourteen

It has been a day of distractions—a patient in trouble who needed some extra time; a meeting at Berkeley to plan a retirement party for a colleague; a couple of manuscripts to read and criticize for friends; and a growing concern about Aunt Lil, the woman who became my surrogate mother when my own mother disappeared, who has been failing. All of which kept me from my own work. Now, as I'm drifting off to sleep, I think about what I owe my aunt, about the twists and turns in our relationship over the years, about my guilt because I haven't been in touch enough recently.

She's calling to me from what seems to be a great distance. She's holding out her hand, stretching it as far as she can in the hope that I can reach her. But no matter how hard I try, I can't quite make it. Our fingers touch and slip away—once, twice, three times—until finally I watch helplessly as she becomes totally unmoored and floats off into space.

The phone wakes me, and I glance at the clock: six-thirty. She died; I know it with a knowledge that's as certain as death itself. I want to pull the blanket over my head, shut out the noise, pretend I don't know what I know. Instead, I put the phone to my ear and listen to my aunt's companion tell me that she died last night. I sit in the middle of my rumpled bed and cry bitter tears for this woman who was such a central actor in my early life.

From the time I was six until just after my eleventh birthday, Aunt Lil was the good mother I longed for, and I was the daughter she never had. She was the woman I could turn to for comfort and advice, the one I could emulate. Where my mother criticized, she approved; where my mother was mean, she was kind; where my mother rejected, she accepted. Her love sheltered me, healed me, made me believe I could be lovable. It was irresistible; I was drawn to her with the fervor of a lover.

In my research for *The Transcendent Child*, I saw how important surrogates are in the lives of children in difficult and troubled families. In nearly every case someone—a teacher, an aunt, a neighbor, a friend—lent a hand when the child needed it most, an intervention that told the child someone cared, that offered comfort and direction at a moment when there was none. For five years Aunt Lil was that person in my life, an immeasurable gift.

She talked to me about her life, the dreams she once had, the books she was reading, and I drank in her words. She was "a lady," she would declare from time to time, always speaking in her most precise and cultured tones as she instructed me on how to become one, too. She corrected my English, taught me table manners, fretted over me when I wasn't dressed as she would have preferred, reminded me that "a lady never uses perfume unless she has just come out of the bath," an instruction that to this day I cannot violate.

At first my mother was pleased that I had a safe place to go after school. Then, when the depth of my attachment to my aunt became clear to her, she was torn. If I didn't go there, I'd roam the streets by myself all afternoon, a prospect that worried her. But she was jealous of the relationship and bristled when she came home from work to find I'd spent time with Aunt Lil. "You have things to do here," she'd say irritably as she set about finding tasks to keep me home.

There wasn't much she could manufacture because I already did the marketing, started the evening meal as instructed, and cleaned the house—a job I could never do to her satisfaction, no matter how hard I tried. I'd spend each Friday afternoon cleaning our one-room apartment from top to bottom, only to have her arrive at the end of the day, run her finger over the baseboard in the hallway as she walked through the door, and slap me across the face because I'd allegedly left some dust.

I still have no idea what, if anything, she could have found. I wasn't, after all, a stupid kid. After being hit a couple of times, I knew enough to pay particular attention to that spot. But it made no difference in that Friday evening ritual. The experience did mark my later life, however, when, after I married, I became an obsessively compulsive housekeeper, cleaning walls and wood-work every week, finding dust where none existed, searching out dirt as if my mother were still after me, and proudly telling myself that her house was never as clean as mine. My family and friends think I'm still something of a cleanliness nut, but compared to those early years, I'm a model of moderation.

By the time I was ten, my relationship with my aunt was suffering seriously from my mother's jealousy. As the cost of pro-voking my mother escalated at home, I began to visit Aunt Lil less often, dropping in no more than one afternoon a week, some-times less. But the strategy only hurt my aunt and didn't mollify my mother. Eventually they fought a bitter battle that perma-nently alienated them from one another and put an end to the oc-casional meals, the Hanukkah dinners, and the Passover seders we shared at Aunt Lil's house.

No one ever said exactly what the fight was about, perhaps be-cause they never understood themselves all that went into creating the growing hostility between them. But I felt guilty for years, convinced that it was my fault, that if I'd been more circumspect about my relationship with my aunt, if I'd been a better, more lov-ing daughter, my mother wouldn't have been so angry and my aunt so hurt.

I wanted desperately to sustain a relationship with Aunt Lil, however truncated it had to be. But she, like my mother, wanted my undivided loyalty, and much as I loved her, I couldn't give what she asked. In the end, therefore, our relationship sank into the mine field between my mother's jealous wrath and my aunt's sense of betrayal.

It ended abruptly one day when I went to visit, and she told me I was no longer welcome. Just like that. No warning, no discus-sion, just her angry, "After all I've done for you, you owed me more respect."

Respect? What was she talking about? There was no one in the world I loved and respected more. I pleaded with her, asked what I had done, what I could do to make amends, swore I would never do anything to hurt her. She didn't explain and wouldn't be moved. She just stood in the doorway, her teeth clenched, her eyes glittering with angry tears, and told me to go away. I remained at her door long after she closed it, weeping and uncomprehending, a forlorn and bewildered child suffering what felt like another death.

It was forty-five years before she would speak with me again. I had just published *Women of a Certain Age,* a book about midlife women, and was in New York at the start of a tour to publicize it. At dinner with her oldest son, with whom I had reestablished contact a few years earlier, he mentioned that his mother, now widowed, had arrived for a visit from Florida earlier in the day. "I want you to take me to her," I said at once. He demurred, fearing it would upset her, telling me once again that she was as unforgiving now as she had been when we were children. But I wouldn't be put off. "I know I can make her talk to me if you'll give me the chance." Reluctantly, he agreed.

We went to my hotel room, where I picked up a copy of the book and signed it with the inscription, "To the woman who made this possible." Then we went to his house, where he introduced me as a friend from California. I was trembling so hard I could barely speak. All the love I ever felt for her swept over me and shook both body and soul. Not just love, anger too. "Why did you let this happen to us?" I wanted to shout. "How could you not know how much I loved you, how much you meant to me, how much I needed you?" I said nothing, of course; I just took her hand in mine and was momentarily calmed by the feel of the cool, brittleness of her aged skin.

We talked, polite chitchat—her life in Florida, mine in California, what I was doing in New York. That was my cue. "I have a gift for you," I said, handing her the book.

She looked at it admiringly, thanked me courteously, then opened it and saw the inscription. She stared blankly, first at the page, then at me, "You can't be . . . ," she stopped, unable to complete the sentence. "I knew," she gasped, "I knew when I saw you there was something, but I never dreamed . . ." Her words trailed off again.

We stood gazing at each other—silent, unbelieving. I tried to speak, but the years of stored up tears were choking me, and for a long moment I could do nothing but wait for them to fall. A voice inside cried, "I can't stand this; the anguish is too much." But it wasn't just anguish; it was pain so mixed with joy that I couldn't distinguish between the two. Finally, the tears came, bringing release from the lump in my throat and the band that seemed to encircle my heart. I reached out and took my aunt in my arms. "Oh, my dear," she wept, "how I've dreamed of this day."

We kept in touch for the next fifteen years or so. I visited her in Florida; she spent an occasional week with me in California; in between we spoke on the phone from time to time. But she never allowed any serious conversation about why she banished me from her life. Only once, after I commented that many of the lessons she taught were still vivid inside me, did she drop her guard and say bitterly, "But you chose her."

"I was eleven years old, and she was my mother. What else could I have done?" I asked.

"I don't know," she replied with a sigh. "Maybe it just had to be that way." Then, in a gesture that was reminiscent of my childhood, she took my hand in both of hers and said, "Never mind. Why talk about those terrible times? I have you back now, and that's all that matters."

But it was never the same. I'm deeply grateful for those early years, convinced I couldn't have grown to the person I am today without the love and sustenance she offered then. I still love her, but it's a child's love, arrested in an eleven-year-old heart where it festered like a painful boil until I could finally seal it over. Our reunion broke the seal and lanced the boil, releasing some of its poison. But she had forced me to finish growing up without her, and there were too many years of living between then and now, too much we hadn't shared, too many questions that would never be answered. There was no way back to the trusting innocence of our earlier relationship and little but the feelings and memories of those years to sustain the present one.

Now, as I try to integrate the reality of her death, the pain of our earlier separation is vivid again. It was easier in the moment to blame my mother, to believe my wonderful aunt would never have cast me out if my mother hadn't made her so angry. But whatever truth there may have been in my child's fantasy, the reality is that Aunt Lil was the one who abandoned me, not my mother. She, true to her word, didn't send us away but stayed the course through more than her fair share of pain and sorrow.

Chapter Fifteen

Funny things happen on the way to old age—funny and ironic and sad and maddening. For one thing, everyone—the clerk in the store, the bank teller, your new dentist—they all seem so young to you. And maybe because they *are* so young, they begin to treat you as if you're so old. They call you "ma'am" as if you were their grandmother; they talk louder as if you can't hear; they speak condescendingly as if to a child; they explain the obvious that needs no explanation.

Then there's the mail. We old folks are big business now and everyone wants a piece of the action. Today's batch brought a "Dear Friend" note that reminds me that "the average funeral costs over $4,700" and advised me to buy life insurance from the sender's company so that "you can afford to bury your spouse." A few days ago a letter from a new "retirement community" in the city informed me in no uncertain terms that I would soon need its services and warned that I'd better make my reservation now because "the available space is going fast." Then there are all the HMOs that bombard me with admonitions about how I face being "wiped out by the medical costs of old age" if I don't take up their generous offers. And these are just a sampling of the endless flow of junk that's addressed to me as a *senior citizen*—from travel agencies to financial planners—all of them promising to make my old age better and richer.

A friend calls, agitated. "If you're collecting stories about how damnably hard it is to get old in this society, I have one for you."

She's an athletic, robust fifty-nine-year-old who sports a shining head of silver hair, the body of a thirty-year-old, and a face that's only now beginning to show the marks of six decades. Her favorite coffee place announced that it would be selling twenty-five-dollar coffee cards, a kind of pay-in-advance plan. Since she goes there for coffee every day, she thought it a splendid idea. On her next visit, she told the clerk she wanted to join the new program and paid the twenty-five dollars. He went off to do the paperwork and returned a minute or two later holding a card. As he handed it to her, he leaned over the counter and said solicitously, as if speaking to a child, "Now be careful and don't lose this; it's just like money."

"Two days later I went and had my hair dyed," she concludes. "I feel vital, alive, productive, my memory is fully intact, yet people are beginning to behave toward me as if I'm an old person, as if I couldn't understand what it means to buy a Peet's coffee card and that it's money. I was so humiliated I wanted to throttle that young man. I didn't mind when people took me for older than I am because of my gray hair. But when they start treating me as if I'm mentally infirm, that's intolerable."

I'm not collecting horror stories, as my friend suggests, but it's hard to avoid them. Aging, it seems, is the subject of the moment, especially among my women friends and colleagues, perhaps because so many of them have begun to enter their fifties and sixties. So it's no surprise when an E-mail arrives from another friend. She's a lithe and lean fifty-seven-year-old, a woman who is a runner, who works out regularly, and who is also an advanced yoga student. Until now she has been proud of the fact that she hasn't succumbed to the temptation to deny or hide her age. She has worn her gray hair and her wrinkles comfortably, insisting that they're her "mark of distinction." "I don't want to be one of those women with their dye jobs and face lifts that remove every vestige of living from their appearance," she said in a recent E-mail message. "I've earned the lines and the wisdom that comes with them."

Now she writes to tell me a story that has shaken her resolve. "I was on the corner waiting for the light to change, having just walked the two miles from my house and planning to walk back up the hill after I took care of my errands. I guess I was in a reverie and didn't notice immediately that the light had changed, when a young woman came up behind me, put her hand on my arm, and asked if I'd like help crossing the street. I was so stunned I could hardly move. It's true that when I turned to look at her she seemed surprised, but the damage was done. When I finally found my voice, I couldn't contain the consternation and irritation and said, not very politely, that I could still make it across on my own.

"I felt bad when I saw her embarrassment; she was a nice young woman who was trying to be helpful. But I have to admit that the whole thing made me think long and hard about how I look and whether I should do something, especially about my hair."

A few days later Hank and I are sitting in a movie theater waiting for the film to begin and I remember to tell these stories to him. He shakes his head and laughs, but not without a pang. "I know how they felt," he says. "Last week I was counting out some change to pay for something I bought in the hardware store and this kid behind the counter reached over and took the money out of my hand. I looked at him, like what the hell are you doing? But he just shrugged and said, 'It looked like you were having trouble counting it,' as if that was an explanation."

"Did you feel terrible?" I ask my husband who looks ten or fifteen years younger than his years.

"It sure as hell didn't make me feel good to have that little punk think I was too old to count some change," he replies, the irritation he felt then still palpable now. "It makes me wonder how many degrading incidents some poor guy who actually looks like an old man has to suffer?"

I think about his comment and know that I, too, am spared the worst of it because I look so much younger than I am. Which reminds me of another story a friend told me recently. She was attending a wedding and chatting with a group of friends, all of them baby boomers in their late forties and early fifties, when one of the men in the group stopped the conversation, pointed to another circle across the room—gray-haired, portly men and

women, probably my age peers, but looking much older than I—
and said, "Hey, you guys, take a look. Are you aware of the risk
factor here? We're going to turn into them." Everyone laughed,
but they all knew they had looked into a future they didn't want
to see.

I wasn't pleased to notice that it makes me feel good to know
that she separated me from those old people at the wedding, as if
looking young were some grand accomplishment instead of my
genes. I'm not proud of myself, either, when I hear myself telling
people my age just so that I can be reassured by their disbelief. Nor
am I comfortable admitting to myself or others that I have some of
the same patronizing contempt for old people (*old* being all those
who look more like my mother's generation than I do) as that
"punk" my husband encountered in the hardware store.

I understand that these feelings are born in the self-hatred
that's so often the lot of those who are identified with a socially
stigmatized group. As a Jew I struggled for many years against my
own internalized anti-Semitism. As a woman it has taken most of
a lifetime to banish the negative stereotypes of *woman* from my internal life. But this knowledge doesn't make me any more comfortable either with my own age or with my wish to distance myself from those whom age hasn't treated so kindly.

I interrupt my thoughts to come back to my conversation with
Hank. "Why didn't you tell me this story before now?"

He shrugs. "I don't know, maybe because . . . well . . . I don't
really know."

"But it's not because you forgot, is it?"

"No, I guess," he says slowly, as if the words hurt, "I had this
peculiar feeling, like I was ashamed, and I didn't want you to
know."

Then as if to wipe away the admission of shame, he changes
the subject abruptly. "It's funny, I know I'm old but I don't feel
old."

I wonder if I should push him to talk about shame, then decide
he doesn't need my probing right now. So I ask instead, "What
does it mean to feel old?"

"Well, I know my hair is thinning, I've lost some more teeth,

I get tired more easily. All that reminds me that I'm old, but then I do my twenty pushups without breaking a sweat and lift more weight than a lot of guys twenty years younger, and I think, *Yes, I can,* and that feels damn good," he declares, his fist raised in a victory salute.

I smile and reach for his hand, thinking about how quickly denial arrives to ease our anxieties. It's a functional defense, especially as the years close in on us and the choice is either denial or perpetual angst. And Hank, in particular, isn't good at living with the dark side. I, too, tend to move toward the light whenever possible, but it doesn't always come as easily to me. Compared to the ethos of pessimism and fear that surrounded my mother and brother, however, I would seem like the bearer of all things light. My inability or unwillingness (either or both) to join them in the darkness was, in fact, one of the things that separated me from them when I was growing up. It was as if my natural optimism, my ability to see a half-full glass where they saw only a half-empty one, was an affront to their sensibilities, a challenge to the certainty of doom in which their dark vision mired them.

Yet it's not only denial that allows my husband to recount his physical feats with pride. Despite our national agony about graying hair, receding hairlines, expanding waistlines, sagging muscles, and failing memories, older is getting younger all the time. When Gloria Steinem turned fifty and people couldn't believe it because she looked so young and beautiful, she quipped, "This is what fifty looks like." It's true about seventy and eighty as well. I look at Hank and think: He doesn't look eighty. But, in fact, this is what eighty looks like now—and how it feels, as well—at least for significant numbers of us. And how we look and feel makes a big difference in how we see ourselves, how we experience our aging, what it means to us, and what options for living seem possible.

The dramatic lengthening of life span over the course of the last hundred years—from forty-seven at the beginning of the century to nearly eighty as we approach its end—has changed the face of old age. For one thing, middle age lasts a lot longer and old age has gotten older. In 1900 only half of all Americans who reached the age of twenty lived to see sixty-five. Now sixty-five is young and one hundred no longer seems just a wistful dream. In fact, people over one hundred are the fastest growing segment of our population, with the eighty-somethings running a close second.

Measured in evolutionary time, this near doubling of our life span is nothing less than a demographic miracle—an astonishing, exhilarating, frightening miracle—that has brought with it a striking change in our concept of old age, along with new concerns about getting old. If fifty-year-olds can expect to live to eighty or more, the question of what to do with those years, how we will live them productively, comes center stage. For those of us who are already here, this is uncharted territory, an unexpected gift of life that can sometimes feel like a blessing, sometimes like a curse, as we search for the path to take us through the thicket of the unknown.

Meanwhile, the visible expressions of the new look of aging are everywhere. The blue-tinted gray-haired, buxom matron of my mother's generation has been replaced by a trim blonde dressed in jeans, running shoes, and a T-shirt. Fifty-eight-year-old Tina Turner, dressed like a teenager, appears triumphantly in the pages of the *New York Times;* the same newspaper publishes a story about "start-over dads" that celebrates, among others, the actor Tony Randall, who became a first-time father at seventy-seven; in the personals column of a San Francisco paper, an "all-around nice guy" in his "early 60s" advertises for a woman "young enough to have a baby or two" because he "wants to be a dad again"; and the news of a sixty-three-year-old first-time mother leaves us caught between astonishment and a yawn, marveling at what science can achieve and already waiting for word of the next "miracle."

If we feel different, we want to be different. The antiaging industry, once the province of the rich few, has become a multibillion-dollar enterprise and a significant part of the nation's economy. Newspapers and magazines feature story after story about how to beat the aging crunch. Health food stores are big business; the gym, once the province of jocks and weight lifters, is now filled with sweating women and men—many of them well into their fifties, sixties, and beyond—trying, with some success, to hold back the ravages of time. For men there's Rogaine to combat hair loss, Clairol to hide the gray, Viagra for impotence, and testosterone treatments as well as a variety of other hormone-based regimens that hold out hope for increased energy, heightened libido, rippling abs, and bulging biceps. For women there's a staggering array of cosmetic and health food store nostrums to augment the promise of estrogen replacement therapy. When all else fails, the surgeon's scalpel comes to the rescue. The American Academy of Cosmetic Surgery reports a mind-boggling increase in plastic surgeries, with men now accounting for one third of all of them, compared with 10 percent just fifteen years ago.

With these thoughts buzzing around in my head, I go to my friend Katherine's baby shower—a women's event where we'll celebrate Katherine's pregnancy and welcome her into the world of mothers. Altogether an unremarkable affair, except that this is the first pregnancy of a forty-nine-year-old woman. As Katherine wanders around the room greeting her guests, she seems suffused in a golden glow of joy. One hand keeps finding her swollen belly and rubbing it rhythmically in small circles, as if she can't wait to touch the infant who lies sleeping in her womb.

Most of the women at the party are around Katherine's age, but their family lives are as different as the times we live in are from those of previous generations. Katherine's sister, younger by three years, has two children in their late teenage years. One early forties woman has a two-year-old; another, just a few years older, has children twenty-six and twenty-eight. There are grandmothers who are the same age as women with six-, seven-, and eight-year-olds.

As I take in this extraordinary display of diverse lifestyles among this group of forty- and fifty-somethings, I'm struck by the fact that, for the first time in history, age is no longer a predictor of life stage for a very large number of Americans. When the life span was so much shorter than it is today, it made sense for people to marry and have children when they were young enough to be reasonably certain they'd live to launch them into adulthood.

When, as is true now, what was once the whole of life is only about half of it, forty doesn't seem too old to have a first child, and fifty, or even sixty, can seem like a beginning, a chance at another adulthood with which to do what we will. And this time, one that comes when, we may be allowed to hope, we have learned from the mistakes of our first adulthood.

I look across the room at Katherine's mother, the only woman there who's close to my age, and think, "She doesn't look seventy." Amused, I remind myself that this is what seventy looks like now. But old habits of thought die hard. Later when we talk, she tells me that, although she works less than in earlier years, she still keeps at least one professional hand in. She's much more interested, however, in talking about her tennis game, a pursuit she took up at sixty. Now, in her middle seventies, she proudly reports that she wins most of the tournaments she enters.

That night the old crone returns. She has been a vague presence in my dream life for several months, felt but not known, agitating my nights but slipping away as soon as consciousness returns. Now she comes again in fully recognizable form, this time meeting me on a flat, dry, nearly barren plain that surrounds what looks like a deep chasm.

As before she's blocking my way, dancing and weaving in front of me so that I can't get by. She looks a little different, cleaner, less mangy, altogether not so grotesque as the last time we met. I try to get past her, but she clutches my arm and laughs. Not the frightening cackle I remember from our earlier meeting but a genuine laugh, as if she's pleased with herself. I flinch when she touches me and brush her off, but she just keeps dancing around and moving backward, her finger beckoning me to follow her to the edge of the ravine.

I'm curious about what's down there but also somewhat acrophobic, so I approach the edge tentatively. She wants me to join her in climbing down the steep, rocky slope. I pull back and she holds out her hand as if she understands that I can't look down without holding something to steady myself. I pull away angrily, repelled by the thought of her touch, and reach instead for the branch of a bush a few feet away. Holding on, I take a quick look and see that there's no bottom, just an empty black void. Angrily I shout at her to go away. "Don't you get it? I'm not going anywhere with

*you." She laughs again. "You will," she says as she seems to float effort-
lessly down into the canyon.*

I wake feeling upset and oddly comforted at the same time. She seems more human to me this time, less menacing, but I still think of her as an alien intruder. My mind knows that she's me, the representation of what I fear about old age. But my emotional self refuses to integrate the knowledge, so she remains *she*—the other, separate, distinct, not me.

She stays with me through most of the morning, imposing herself on my thoughts whenever I have a few minutes free. What does she want from me? I know the answer: She wants me to accept my aging, to be kinder to myself and to others, to believe that the precipice on which I stand doesn't lead to a bottomless pit, that the descent will take me to a peaceful valley. But despite the odd moments of acceptance that come to me now, I also know it's a descent, and I'm not ready.

I sometimes think that life is the perfect Jewish joke—a joke that underscores the incongruity of the tragic and absurd that live side by side in life's satire. The great Jewish writers and comics have always understood this in their *kishkas* (literally, intestines). It's what enables them to show up this gift of life for what it is: a gift that comes with strings, not least of them that everything we care about—including life itself—eventually will be taken from us.

Yes, it's a bad joke. At the very moment when the tasks and obligations of life are done, when we have learned to appreciate ourselves and our lives most fully, when we are more at peace than ever before and ready to live life more expansively, we're expected to sit by and watch ourselves fade slowly but inexorably into a diminished old age. The old crone of my dreams tries to tempt me, to convince me that it's not so bad, that it's possible to glide effortlessly down into the canyon and find warmth and welcome there. But even if I believed that I could easily navigate the steep, rock-strewn path she showed me, I don't want to go there. I don't want to live in some peaceful valley. I want my life as I know it—full and rich and, yes, with a future that promises more than turning into an old crone.

Chapter Sixteen

I've been in my writer's cave for several weeks now, and my desk is piled high with tasks undone—manuscripts waiting to be read, a couple of articles to referee for professional journals, patients' status reports for their insurance companies, E-mail messages from friends that deserve more than my brief "I'm in my cave and will write when I come up for air" response. So I've spent most of this day clearing away those things that come with a deadline, organizing the rest into orderly piles, and promising myself that they'll all be done before the week is out.

I feel irritated by all these demands, edgy because I didn't get to write until so late in the day and won't be able to accomplish much. I have to smile at these thoughts, at how I keep finding myself in a no-win place. When I'm not busy enough I worry that I'll end my life in idle boredom; when I'm too busy I fret because I have no time for myself; when I'm down in my writing cave I'm upset because I'm shutting out life at a time when there's not much of it left; when I'm not writing my life feels empty and I fear my brain has atrophied.

I think about my mother and wonder if getting old was as hard for her as it is for me. In her later years her life seemed empty and pointless to me, but I have no idea whether she felt that way. Maybe it's like my friend Dorothy says about beauty: You can't mourn it if you never had it. Maybe living out a dull and uninteresting old age isn't so hard if you never felt your life to be vital and engaged before. Or is that elitist nonsense, the narcissistic fantasy of someone who needs to believe in the specialness of her life and the uniqueness of her struggles?

I wonder, as I recall our lives together, who she really was, whether even now I understand the demons that drove her or know what gave her pleasure. There were occasional men in her life when we were younger. One, Henry, was around for a year or so when I was about nine years old until, like everyone else who entered my mother's life, he disappeared and we were never allowed to mention him again. He was a quiet, kind man, and I liked him, but my mother's behavior in his presence made me wary and uncomfortable. Her flirtatious smiles embarrassed me and her sudden small kindnesses to me were, I knew from experience, an act that would disappear as soon as the door closed behind him.

I didn't exactly know what sex was yet, but the street world had already taught me it was something dirty. So I was stricken when I came home from school early one day and found them in the bedroom guiltily gathering their clothes around them. Confused and mortified, I fled to Aunt Lil's and refused to go home until the next day, when my mother came and dragged me back.

Thinking about my behavior then, I'm struck by the cruelty of children and the child's narcissism that kept me from seeing anything but my own concerns. My mother's loneliness, her hunger for companionship, for sex—none of this entered my nine-year-old mind. I knew only that she had done something dirty, and that I was deeply, profoundly ashamed. I suppose a child today, having been raised in the kind of open sexual environment that surrounds us now, wouldn't experience the overt expression of a parent's sexuality with so much drama. But then, if we knew anything at all about sex, it was only that it was dirty, disgusting, *yiccchhh,* not, we would assure ourselves, something our parents would ever do.

What would my mother remember about all this? Or more to the point, what would be her version of these and other events in our past? I see with my own daughter, with whom I'm so close, how our memories of our shared lives can sometimes be different.

Such discrepancies are natural, of course, part of the different ways we each filter and internalize experience. But it can be disconcerting to know that someone with whom your life has been so closely joined sees the same event so differently that she writes a whole other story. For my mother, such discrepancies were nearly intolerable, which is why the phrase "It never happened" rings so frequently and powerfully in my ears.

When I wrote in the introduction to *Worlds of Pain,* my first book about working-class family life, that I learned in my own family about "illness, death, and poverty, about the struggle to survive, and about the toll it takes on family life," she responded with fury when my brother read those words to her. "You sure made Mom mad telling the world we were poor," he reported as we expressed our astonishment over her version of our lives. I waited a couple of weeks to phone her, hoping by then she'd have forgotten, but she greeted me with renewed rage. "How could you say we were poor?" she demanded. "You always had everything you needed, didn't you?" No words, no reminders of past events mollified her; she stuck to her story that we were a nice middle-class family who always had everything we needed.

Given the stigma that attaches to poverty in America, it's understandable that my mother would want to deny that this was her lot. We all tend to rewrite our history somewhat to make it more congruent with how we want to present ourselves to the world and what we would have liked our lives to be. This has always been one of the barriers between my mother and me: I have little talent for that kind of denial, and her insistence on it made me feel crazy at times. In adulthood, I learned to find others to provide the reality checks I needed, but as a child, her denial was the source of many of our fights as I struggled to retain a toehold in reality.

The one thing my mother and I would agree on is that the election of Franklin Delano Roosevelt in 1932 was a crucial turning point in the life of our family, although I certainly didn't understand it that way when it first happened. In my mother's mind, FDR was "good for the Jews," which made anything he did fine with her. Even when, after World War II, it became clear that

Roosevelt had joined his anti-Semitic State Department in refusing asylum to the European Jews who were being slaughtered in
Hitler's concentration camps, she held fast to her insistence that he
was good for the Jews.

I wasn't so concerned about the Jews (we didn't know yet
about Hitler's plan of extermination) but, within a few years after
FDR ascended to the presidency, the social programs he put in
place helped to lift us out of the worst of our poverty. We still fell
out of the working poor and on to the welfare rolls at times, but
painful as that was, at least there was help. More important for the
long term, his National Industrial Recovery Act (NIRA), which
became law in 1933, included a clause that gave renewed life and
energy to the trade union movement. For the first time, the
United States government guaranteed the right of unions to organize. Which also meant that workers couldn't be fired for joining
a union.

When the law went into effect, only a small fraction of New
York's garment workers were members of the ILGWU. Organizing efforts, which had been stalled by earlier factional fights,
were further hampered by the Depression, which made workers
even more fearful than before about engaging in any union activity that could cost them their jobs. Now, with the law on its side,
the union called a general strike of garment workers in New York
City. Seventy thousand workers shut down the entire industry.
My mother was not among them.

To her, the union leaders were just another bunch of thugs
who wanted to put their hands in her pocket. No matter what they
promised, she "knew" they were up to no good. And she certainly
wasn't ready to part with any of her hard-won earnings to pay
union dues. "They're a bunch of gangsters," she'd say dismissively
as she related their efforts to recruit her.

But the union would not be denied. The strike was a triumph
that solidified its power over the industry and changed the lives of
garment workers forever. Unionization didn't bring paradise, but
working conditions in the industry were improved beyond anything the workers could have imagined in the past. Wages in-

creased by as much as 50 percent; the standard work week dropped to thirty-five hours, with overtime pay for more than that; grievance procedures were established to protect workers from unfettered exploitation. Most important for the life and health of the union, most factories in New York were closed shops, meaning that a worker had to be a union member to get a job. By the time the Supreme Court declared the NIRA unconstitutional in 1935, the union's power was firmly entrenched.

It's one of the tragic costs of illiteracy that news travels more slowly to those who can't read or write. So it took a long time for my mother to realize that the union was changing the face of the industry in which she worked. There was word of mouth, of course, a normally efficient means of communication, especially at the workplace. But the nonunion shop in Long Island City where my mother worked was enough outside the mainstream so that the word didn't penetrate its walls for a while. To the degree that it did, my mother would have been the last to hear it because she kept such a wary distance from people around her. I don't mean that she never took part in some of the bawdy banter that characterized the interaction among the women she worked with. But she generally had little time or inclination for anything she considered frivolous. And gossiping with her co-workers before or after work was high on her list of unnecessary frivolities.

Eventually, however, the news filtered through to her and, once she understood what was happening, she acted quickly and decisively. She still didn't like the unions, still wasn't wholly convinced that they were really working for people like her, still snorted derisively *ganevim* (crooks) whenever she talked about them. But her fussing and fuming notwithstanding, the next time a union representative came around to sign her up, she agreed to pay her dues if they found her a job in Manhattan.

That move changed her from hostile skeptic to ardent unionist as they demonstrated their power by getting her the job she'd asked for at wages that were far more than what she had been earning. Right up to her death, my mother never stopped worrying about money, never gave up her careful ways, never spent a dime she didn't have to. But the one bill she paid without a grumble was her union dues, a membership she kept up for years after she retired. For the rest of her life, the union movement was the one progressive cause she supported unswervingly.

For me, living through the organization of New York's garment workers, experiencing firsthand how the union movement touched and changed my family's life, was the beginning of my political understanding, providing an education in the power of collective action I would never forget. Many years later, when I became a political activist and organizer, it was the lessons I learned as a child about the importance of collective action in bringing about social change that fueled the energy and conviction I brought to my work.

Even with the gains made by the union, however, the life of a garment worker—especially one like my mother, whose unskilled work was at the lowest level of the wage hierarchy—didn't become a walk on the sunny side of the street. True, her wages and working conditions improved dramatically. The increase in pay and decrease in working hours meant that in thirty-five hours a week she earned about as much as she had in forty-four or fifty. If she put in extra hours, she got overtime pay; if she had a grievance, the shop steward was there to listen.

With all that, however, we were still poor; she still worked in a factory doing what she called *shmutzike arbeit* (dirty work); she still struggled to pay the bills; and the approach of the slack season still filled us with dread. The big change was that we were no longer in such imminent danger of tumbling over the edge of the precipice, partly because of the changes the union wrought but also because the New Deal legislation of the Roosevelt years provided a safety net for families in need.

It was then that what we know now as the modern welfare state came into being, first with the Federal Emergency Relief Administration (FERA), later with Aid to Dependent Children (ADC), the first national program designed to assist widows with young children. Until then there had been poor relief, mean subsidies administered capriciously by local jurisdictions to people they defined as "the deserving poor." Now, for the first time, the federal government joined the cities and states in assuming some share of the responsibility for poor families who couldn't make it on their own.

For my mother these new federal programs provided the first small bit of security she had ever known. Later there would be un-employment insurance to tide her over the worst effects of being out of work. But in the first years of the New Deal there were only these public assistance programs to which she could turn when slack season rolled around again.

Welfare! I listen to the mean-spirited discussions about welfare now, to the endless talk about the value of self-reliance by people who will never know the shame of being in need no matter how reliable you have been, and I want to shout, "How dare you? What do you know about being relegated to the lowest paid work this society has to offer? What do you know about working to the point of exhaustion and still not earning enough to feed and clothe a family? What do you know about being called out of your fifth grade class by a social worker who has come to check on the story your mother has told?"

It's unforgettable—the agony of that walk to the front of the room with all eyes upon me, the humiliation when I saw my teacher's obvious concern, the tears that stung the back of my eyes as I struggled for control, the fear that everyone would know my shame. It was bad enough to be the only child in the class who had no father; now everyone would know how poor we were as well. School, which had been my haven, my place of retreat, became, in that moment, my hell.

My mother had warned me that this might happen—warned me and coached me to be sure I was ready with the right answers. Like so many poor women seeking welfare, she sometimes did some work on the side to supplement the inadequate dole. She'd alter some clothes for a neighbor or work a few hours at a local shop doing small alterations like putting cuffs on pants or hem-ming a skirt. My job, if I was asked, was to know nothing of these activities, to say only that she was unemployed.

Lying, however, has never been my strong point, and I did it even less well as a child. So I was frightened by the whole idea and pleaded with her not to make me do it. But she was determined to collect her due, even if she had to bend the rules to get it. There was no way out for me.

Later I came to understand that such lies are part of the survival strategies of the poor, that people who feel abused and victimized by society often find it hard to play by its rules. I understand, too, that for my mother, there was an element of retribution every time she foiled the system in some way. When she lost the money from my father's life insurance policy in the bank failures of 1932, she was left with a deep-seated sense of injury, a conviction that the system had failed her and that, therefore, she was entitled to wrest from it what she could. And she did, whether in small ways like pushing her children under the subway turnstile instead of paying their fares, even after we were half grown; or in larger ways like working insurance scams where she would threaten suit for some injury, usually contrived—nuisance threats that the insurance companies often settled for some paltry sum, perhaps twenty or twenty-five dollars, that looked huge to my mother's impoverished and triumphant eyes.

As a child, I was embarrassed by these things she did and lived in fear that she or we would get caught. So as I walked to the principal's office, I was angry at my mother for making me do this while I also nervously tried to remember what she told me to say. What if I didn't get it right?

I don't know what image I'd conjured in my mind about the social worker before we met, but when I finally sat down before her, I was surprised by her soft, gentle voice and the warmth and kindness she displayed. But the questions! "Is your mother working?" "When was the last time she worked?" "What does she do all day?" "What did you eat for dinner last night?" They left me squirming with guilt and dread.

What were the right answers? Nobody told me she'd ask what I ate for dinner. Or what my mother did all day. I didn't know exactly when she last worked. What if I made a mistake? What if I slipped and told that my mother earned some extra money by sewing things for other people? What would happen to us? What would my mother do to me?

I must have gotten the answers right because we were approved for relief. But it took quite a while before I was comfortable in school again, before I could stop wondering what the other kids knew, what my teacher was thinking. And I was well into adulthood before I was able to put behind me the stigma of those years when we would fall out of the working poor and on to the welfare rolls.

If my mother could read these words, she'd be furious, calling me a liar and denying that any of this ever happened. A part of me smiles now at her need to change history and understands that it's in the service of maintaining her fierce pride, her belief in her independence, and most of all, a defense against the knowledge that she couldn't give her children a better life than she had. I want to say to her, "It's okay, Mom, you don't have to be ashamed; it's a society that doesn't care for its weakest members that should hang its head in shame." To which I'm certain she'd snap back, "Hnnnph, so you're still talking that Communist *chazerei* (garbage); I thought you'd have grown up by now."

Chapter Seventeen

I'm visiting my close friends, Michael and Amy, in New York when out of nowhere I find myself holding a naked, newborn little girl. She squirms around in my arms, her hands and legs flailing about so urgently that I'm afraid I'll drop her, so I put her on the bed and stand looking down at her in bewilderment. Where did she come from? What do I do with her? I know I have to do something, but I can't figure out what.

I feel terrible watching her fretful thrashing but I'm helpless to calm her. Finally, Amy hears the noise and comes into the room. "Maybe if we dress her she'll feel quieter," she says. To my astonishment I react to her words as if I've never heard of dressing a baby before.

Finally, I pull myself together, grab hold of the baby firmly, and ask Amy, who is about to have a child and is well stocked with baby necessities, for some clothes. She goes off to get a diaper, but she can't find one. She mutters to herself, trying to figure out where she might have put the diapers, while Michael runs around searching the house. Finally, he comes back with a diaper, but it's such a strange contraption that I have no idea how to put it on. Amy takes it from me and tries, but she isn't any more successful than I am.

After several tries Michael finally gets the thing to work and goes to bring the rest of the clothes. He comes back with pants and shirt that are huge. I ask them for something smaller but he says this is all they have. It doesn't make sense. I know they have some tiny garments waiting for their baby; they showed them to me when I arrived. But I'm afraid to ask again because I'm uncomfortable about imposing on them and worried that they're tired of me and this baby and just want us to go away.

I wrestle the baby into the pants that are many sizes too big for her, but I can't get the shirt on because I can't find the opening for the head. I run my hands around the inside of the shirt, pushing and poking for an opening, but it's not there. Frustrated, I think: How did I get this baby anyway; I don't want her in my life; it's not the right time.

I awaken remembering an earlier vivid new baby dream in which she arrived fully clothed and, no matter how hard I tried, I couldn't get her undressed. Now the baby is naked, and I know at once that there's a connection between the two. But before I can think about it, I find myself intrigued by the machinations of the mind, by what it remembers and what it forgets. For in the month or two between these two dreams I had several other new baby dreams in which the imagery was obscure and faded as soon as I woke up, leaving only the knowledge that there was a baby in the dream. Yet I never connected them to that earlier dream. Instead I was satisfied with a more facile interpretation that assumed that the baby in those opaque dreams represented this book which, at times, seems to me like a baby in the womb, unformed and insubstantial.

But this dream is different, fuller, more assertive, with a message that demands my attention. I lie there quietly for some minutes while its impact sinks into my consciousness and the words *It's not the right time* reverberate in my mind. Not the right time for what? Certainly it's not about writing this book.

Suddenly I know the answer, the one I haven't wanted to know, still don't want to know, the one my unconscious is now forcing upon me. The clothed baby dream told me that, to live a new season well, I have to shed the heavy garments of the past and be willing at least to see what might emerge without their constraints. Now the clothes are gone; I have only this naked infant. She comes into the world unformed, uncivilized, unclothed, unskilled, as all babies do, and she needs me to mother her. Friends and family, no matter how well meaning, can offer sympathy and support, but it's a job I alone must do. Only when I'm ready to care for her properly—to take her into my heart, to nurture her lovingly, and yes, to dress her appropriately—will she stop her flailing around in helpless agony.

I get the message and I understand now that, like it or not, it *is* the right time. But I'm still uncertain about what kind of clothes I need.

This is one of my clinical days and I have to be at my office in an hour, so I pull myself out of bed and away from the dream. But it nags at me throughout the day. It's not the first time in my life I've felt that I was giving birth to a new self, or at least to a part of myself that was unknown before. The changes I've undergone over the years seem so profound to me that the person who's now reaching old age bears only the slightest resemblance to the child in my family, or even to the young wife and mother of my first marriage. But it's surely one of life's more curious ironies that growing old means birthing and nurturing yet another new self, only this time one that's guaranteed only a brief life span.

At home in the early evening I sit with Hank sipping a before-dinner glass of wine and watching the sun sink into the fog bank that has settled itself outside the Golden Gate. We're quiet for some minutes as we watch the sky turn yellow, pink, purple, and finally a deep vibrant crimson. In the silence my mind skips about from thought to thought, as if trying to shut out the dream. "Sometimes when I look out over the ocean like this," I finally say, "I feel like I did as a child when I imagined that if I looked hard enough I could see all the way to China."

"Are you saying you feel like a child now?" he asks.

"I don't know, but I dreamed I had a baby last night," I reply, and launch into the telling of the dream and my interpretation.

He listens attentively. When I finish he can't seem to find words, so he says simply, "I wish this aging thing wasn't so hard for you."

I sigh, trying not to let my impatience show. Most of the time the calm quiet with which he approaches life, his philosophical acceptance, soothes my more volatile nature. But now I want to shake him out of that calm. I need to feel as if he can join me in this walk into old age, and in this moment it feels as if he's standing apart. "I don't understand you. How can you be so easy about getting old?" I say, unable to keep my irritation in check.

We've had this conversation before, so before he can speak the words, I interject, "Don't say, 'What else is there to do but to accept it?' I know there's nothing else to do, but that doesn't stop me from wanting to shake my fists and shout at the heavens. I don't get it. Don't you ever feel that way? Or are you content to spend the rest of your life hiding from yourself and your feelings?"

I'm appalled at my words. Why do I have to batter down his denial? Will it make me feel any better to know he's struggling as much as I am? Before I can speak again, he says, his own impatience now showing, "No, you don't understand. I don't think I'm in denial; I'm very aware of my aging and I have the same concerns about it as you do. I notice my forgetfulness as well as you do, and I probably like it even less. There's nothing to like about getting old and coming to terms with your waning powers. And it scares the hell out of me to think about living a diminished life. But meanwhile I'm healthy and in command of my senses, and I won't ruin today by worrying about the future."

"Do you think my concerns about tomorrow ruin my todays?"

"I don't know, but they certainly don't make them easy, either for you or for me."

"That's true, but that doesn't mean they're ruined. In some ways it's the opposite. They may be more precious to me because I'm so aware how few of them are left. And all I really want out of each day—hard as it may make them—is to feel everything as fully as I can; that's what being alive means to me."

His momentary irritation slips away and he puts his arm around my shoulder, pulls me toward him, and says gently, "Yes, I know, but it's not what makes me feel alive, and after all these years you know that's not going to change. You can stamp your foot and shout at the heavens, but that's not my way. You're the one who keeps saying people don't change when they get old, they just get more of the same. Well . . . ?"

Later that evening I send an E-mail to an old friend in Florida, with whom I correspond frequently. Over the years we have talked about aging from time to time, sharing our feelings, think-

ing about where we've been, where we're going, how we'll manage the next stage. He's a sixty-eight-year-old gay man in a long-
term, stable relationship who contests with his own aging by playing a fierce game of tennis, walking miles along the beach with his
dog, and working out every day.

I recount my dream and reflect on its meaning. He responds at
once, saying my interpretation is "right on," and reminds me that
I live with a man who is the very model of how to accept aging.
"It seems to me the answer to your how-does-one-live-at-this-
stage-of-the-game resides in your very own house. Hank's way
is the only way I know. One just keeps on keeping on doing the
things that give pleasure in the doing of them. I know that's right
although it doesn't make it any easier. I understand so little about
what I am now going through. It seems to me that my youth has a
hold on my mind that gets in the way of wisdom."

I write back saying, "I've just had that conversation with the
man I live with, and you're right; he's the model of how to do this.
But I fear we each have to find our own way, as he just reminded
me, and his way isn't mine. Sometimes when my struggle with this
whole aging business feels particularly hard, I wish his way were
mine. But even as I think that I know I really don't mean it. I expect you might be thinking that's because I like the suffering, but
I don't think that's right. It's more that feeling it all—the pain as
well as the pleasure—is what makes me feel fully alive and to cir-
cumvent those feelings, even if I could, seems to me like giving up
on life. As for youth having a hold on your mind, as you can see,
it's old age that seems to have gripped mine and, for the moment
at least, won't let go."

He responds with a story about meeting a "young man, perhaps thirty, intensely good-looking in that South Florida way,
black hair, tiger eyes, all that stuff" who made a pass at him.
"What's weird about this odd encounter," he concludes, "is that it
raised all kinds of memories and longings I associate with being
young and crazy. But since this romantic scene is nothing I want
in my life, at least not consciously, I wonder why I have thought
about it repeatedly since it happened."

I reply, saying that I believe the incident touched him so because part of him yearns to feel the kind of pure sexual passion that motivated the young man who accosted him. He tells me I'm "absolutely right," then goes on to say, "One of the things that troubles me most about my age is that the old passions have faded. There was a time when I would have had at least a weekend of wild, crazy stuff with that guy, but not anymore. Not even if I wanted to would I do it. There is the consideration of Michael's feelings certainly. But more there is the consideration of my own. I know all the lines, can imagine the sensations, and I don't want them anymore, partly because those sorts of feelings carry with them inevitable pain I can no longer manage."

"Is that what getting old is about, the fear of pain, the unwillingness to risk?" I ask in my next note.

"Hey, kid, it's not so bad. You may need the Sturm und Drang, but I kind of cherish the placid quality of my life now," he replies, putting an end to this extended E-mail conversation but not to my thoughts, especially about fading passions.

The muted experience my husband and I share now is a weak shadow of the sexual charge that, for so many years, ran like an electric current between us. It's true that our sexual encounters remain deeply intimate and pleasurable experiences, perhaps more intimate now than before, when urgency drove us. But when I read some of the glowing articles about sex in old age that have begun to appear recently, about how much better it can be because the urgency is gone, I wonder whether the writers ever felt the thrill of sexual desire that demands satisfaction.

It isn't only sexual passion I miss, although obviously that's no small part of the loss. Old age brings with it a kind of moderation, a restraint, as if a conservator has been appointed to husband the body's fading energy. *Moderation and restraint!* Until now these have been alien words, unthinkable thoughts, although admittedly I've sometimes wished I didn't have to live with the kind of passionate intensity that has always driven me before. But now as I watch that ebb away, I'm saddened by the loss and confused about what I really want because there's a small but growing part of me that feels relieved to be less driven, less intense, while the other mourns for who I was and worries about what I will become.

I recall my naked baby dream and wonder: What are the right clothes for this stage of my life? How do I find them? I think about some of the women in my therapy practice—forty-somethings who gave up whatever early career aspirations they may have had to become stay-at-home moms. Now, they come into therapy feeling naked, vulnerable, and searching for the wardrobe to take them into next stage of their lives. Why is it so easy for me to help them find solutions, while I thrash about feeling frightened and befuddled? I can hear my former therapist saying, "It's the *idea* of old age that's so threatening for you, not the reality." But that's not wholly true. For in this case the idea and the reality are very closely entwined, and the task is to come to terms with the daunting reality of old age and all it means while I find the way to move into this next stage of my life with more grace than I've been able to muster until now.

Chapter Eighteen

It's the first night of Hanukkah, two years since my mother died and just weeks before my seventy-fifth birthday. Marci turned fifty a few months ago, and I'm coming up on seventy-five. I'm not sure which is harder to integrate.

We're at Marci's, as we have been for the last two years on this night, preparing for our *latke* dinner. I'm peeling mountains of potatoes, Hank is weeping over the onions, and Marci is being all-around helper while she sets the table for the twelve friends who will be here soon.

I love this ritual meal that's now a part of our lives, and I feel my mother's presence on this day differently than I usually do. It's as if in death she left me this gift, this small, joyful celebration of my Jewishness, that I didn't have before. I don't mean that I haven't always identified as a Jew, only that I've been such a secular one that I haven't attended much to the rituals and ceremonials of Judaism. My thoughts go back to the day of her death, to my notion, half-believed, that she contrived to die on Christmas Eve so that I could never again fully enjoy the holiday. Now I think, "She took Christmas but gave me Hanukkah; it's not such a bad exchange."

As I peel and grate, my thoughts take me back to the years when anti-Semitism was a powerful force in my life, and I wonder now whether some of my distance from the lore of Judaism was born in my ambivalence about bearing this stigmatized identity. For I have known deep in my soul the meaning of what we in the tribe contemptuously call Jewish self-hatred.

I watch my daughter as she bustles about, amazed and grateful that she seems to have none of that ambivalence, probably because she was brought up in a different world from the one I knew in my early years. Then there were still Jewish quotas at most colleges and universities in the country; there were still neighborhoods, hotels, social clubs, fraternities, and sororities from which Jews were excluded, and there was still discrimination in the workplace where Jews were barred from many different kinds of jobs, including even the lowly ones for which my high school training qualified me.

I was fifteen years old when I graduated from high school in 1939 and went in search of my first full-time job. I'd had only one job before then—part-time clerical work in the summer between my junior and senior high school years—largely because there was little work available for teenage girls. Baby-sitting, the most common employment opportunity for girls today, didn't exist in the community I lived in. People simply didn't go out without their children, at least not until they were old enough to be left on their own. Clerking in the local stores wasn't an option either because they were almost all family enterprises, mom-and-pop stores where parents carried the main load and kids filled in as needed.

My brother worked as a delivery boy all through our childhood and adolescence, but delivering groceries was out of the question for a girl. That was boys' work. It's not that anyone ever said that; they didn't have to. It was a fact of life, part of the role distinctions of the time that might as well have been written in the genes. Girls not only didn't deliver groceries, it didn't occur to us to question the rule.

Finding a job for anyone wasn't easy in the closing years of the Depression, but for a fifteen-year-old Jewish girl it was a real problem. Even though I had a high school diploma, the law in New York said I was too young to work without working papers. Since I assumed no one would hire a fifteen-year-old, even with working papers, I simply lied about my age. I didn't know yet that it wasn't the only lie I'd have to tell to get a job.

Since I was a pretty kid who also came with reasonably good

stenography and typing skills, I looked, at first glance, like the kind of applicant who would be easy to place. So I was welcomed when I walked into an employment agency and asked about a job. "Yes, I think we have something for you; just fill in this application while I go through the files," the woman behind the desk said brightly after a brief interview.

But those were the days when applications routinely inquired about religion and the warm welcome turned icy as soon as she saw the word *Jewish*. The smile vanished, the eyes grew distant, the promise of a job moments before suddenly turned into a vague, "I'll keep your application on file and let you know."

I knew about anti-Semitism before this, of course. I had been brought up on stories of Russian pogroms, of Jewish babies being thrown in the air and caught on the bayonets of Cossack soldiers. Even in the small corner of the world I grew up in, where the kids didn't discriminate when they screamed epithets like *wop, kike,* or *mick* at each other, I knew that we Jews were seen as a breed apart. And if ever there was a doubt, it vanished as soon as we reached puberty and parents laid down the law against their sons dating a Jewish girl.

Still, until I went job hunting I'd never before had to pay the price of being Jewish so directly. Each time I met that cold rejection, each time the promise of a job vanished before my bewildered eyes, I'd leave feeling angry, humiliated, and worst of all, helpless. There was nowhere to turn, no one to hold my hand. When I'd come home and try to talk to my mother about these experiences, she'd give me one of her "educated dope" looks and shrug. "What, you didn't know this is a *goyishe* world?" Or "You, with the fleas in the nose [her version of high and mighty], maybe you thought you'd be different?"

I'd walk away from those exchanges feeling lost, alone, and stupid for looking to her for aid or comfort, and I soon learned to keep my own counsel. When, at the end of the day, she'd come home and say, "So, did you find anything yet?" I simply said no and went back to my book or whatever else I was doing. But I needed a job. So after weeks of bumping up against the same warm reception followed by a chilly rejection, I changed my name from Breslow to Preston and wrote *Protestant* in the box that asked for my religion. Within days I had a job.

I was afraid to tell my mother what I'd done, fearful that she'd see it as a heinous crime against her God—not mine, since I had long ago stopped believing. I should have known better. It's true that being Jewish was at the core of her identity, but she was also a very canny, pragmatic woman. *"Un abrerruh hust du?"* (What choice do you have?) was all she would say when I told her. Later, when I tried to get her to talk to me, perhaps to help me with my guilt about what I'd done, she responded edgily, "What's to talk about? If that's what it takes to get a job in this America, that's what you do. What? You think God wants you to starve because those anti-Semites run the world?"

This, in fact, was her whole orientation to religion. She claimed to be an Orthodox Jew and invoked God regularly. But she accepted only those rituals of the religion that were convenient and refused the others. We didn't have different dishes for meat and dairy foods; we didn't scrub the house from top to bottom at Passover to get rid of all traces of *chumetz* (banned foods); we didn't go to synagogue on the two most sacred holidays of the year—Rosh Hoshanna and Yom Kippur. Those things, she would say, were for the rich who could afford two sets of dishes and the price of tickets to the synagogue. Even as a child, I could see that this was a realistic adaptation to the circumstances of her life, but I was never fully convinced of her religious conviction.

Marci interrupts my thoughts, "Hey, Mom, you're pretty quiet; what's going on?"

"Have you ever had any direct experience with anti-Semitism?" I ask.

She looks puzzled, clearly wondering what motivates the question, but she indulges me with a direct answer. "No, I mean, I know it's there, and I work in a corporation that doesn't have many Jews, especially in the top jobs. I laughed when I first went to work at the bank because of all the stereotypes about Jews owning the industry. I mean, where are they? But if you're asking if I've felt left out or discriminated against in some way because I'm Jewish,

I don't think so. Or at least I didn't know it if I was. I feel that more as a woman working in the boys' world. But at this stage of my career, I'm sure there's no glass ceiling because I'm Jewish. What's this about, anyway?"

"I've just been thinking about the time when I couldn't get a job because I'm Jewish."

The three of us—Hank, Marci, and I—talk about those days while we work, comparing the differences between now and then. I sometimes wonder how much of Jews' continuing concern about anti-Semitism is real, how much Jewish paranoia. Then I pick up the newspaper and read about some militia groups spouting hatred of blacks and Jews, or see television images of a synagogue that's defaced with swastikas, or listen to the "this-is-a-Christian-country" mantra of the Christian right, and I know that anti-Semitism isn't just a relic of the past, that it's not an either-or question, and that even paranoids have enemies.

The conversation moves naturally to my mother, whose antipathy to me expanded to include my daughter. It started early, when Marci was an infant and would cry and become rigid with fear whenever my mother came near her. My mother, unable to tolerate what felt like a rejection, responded angrily and critically: "There's something wrong with that child," she'd insist irately. "You must be doing something to her to make her like this," she'd announce with certainty. "You and your mother-in-law, you're turning her against me," she'd complain bitterly. But, in fact, I was almost as distressed about Marci's behavior as my mother was.

It's tempting to say that my infant daughter could sense my mother's hard, cruel edge, but who really knows why a baby responds that way. What I do know is that she was fine with others and loved being held by her other grandmother. But until she was several months old, she could barely tolerate my mother's presence, let alone her touch. Later, when she was older and tried to befriend my mother, it never really worked. My mother would sometimes speak the words of a caring grandmother, but the affect to match the words was missing and the critical edge was always present.

"I always felt bad that I couldn't find a way to get to Grandma,"

Marci says. "Once in a while I'd feel like I did, like the time I got her to tell me about the town she was born in and what her life was like. But most of the time she wasn't really interested in talking to me, and it felt like she didn't like me any more than she liked you."

I turn from the sink and put my arms around my daughter. "I wish I could have given you the grandmother you deserve."

She kisses my cheek and quips, "Yeah, and it would have been great if you had the kind of mother you deserve. At least I had Grandma Fanny, who I knew loved me."

Meanwhile I'm struggling with Marci's Cuisinart. "Damnit, next year I'm bringing mine."

"You always say that, then carry on about this one," she retorts, and takes over the task of grating the potatoes and onions. "You know, there's an easier way to get me to do this," she teases, "you could just ask."

I don't think I manipulated her into taking over, but I'm glad to give the task over to her. Hank has finished with the onions and is preparing the chickens, so I go on to fixing the salad. While I search in the refrigerator for the fixings, I return to my musings about being Jewish and consider how different it was for my generation than for those who came later.

At the same time that I was denying my Jewishness, I was watching the world anxiously as anti-Semitism in our own country was fueled by the growing power of Hitler's Germany. Great Britain and France had gone to war in September 1939 when German troops marched unannounced into Poland, and the European Allies finally understood that only a victory on the battlefield would stop Hitler. One by one, the countries of Europe fell with little resistance: Denmark, Norway, Holland, Belgium, Luxembourg, France, Greece, Yugoslavia. Only Great Britain had so far been able to withstand the German onslaught, protected from invasion by the English Channel but suffering a nearly unendurable assault from the air.

It was a difficult time for all Americans, as the uncertain outcome of the war in Europe hung like a cloud over our lives. But it was particularly hard for Jews, who became increasingly frightened by what seemed to be the invincibility of the German war machine and by the widespread belief, fostered and repeated by our homegrown anti-Semites, that Jews were responsible for the approaching war.

With each German victory, the rumors of anti-Semitic atrocities grew louder, although no one was able yet to grasp fully the horror that would come. There was no television then to bring pictures of world events into our living rooms as they were happening. I had only the New York tabloids and the movies, where every performance started with a newsreel. Yet the images of the time are engraved in my memory: German tanks entering Warsaw as the narrator in the newsreel intoned the story of Poland's defeat in just twenty-seven days; Adolf Hitler speaking before tens of thousands of ecstatic Germans, their arms raised in the stiff Nazi salute as they chanted adoringly, *Sieg Heil, Sieg Heil;* German troops strutting around the capitals of Europe like the supermen they believed themselves to be.

Hank interrupts my thoughts, "What got you to thinking about anti-Semitism now?"

I have to stop and think, trying to rerun the tape that set my thinking off. "I'm not sure, maybe because it's Hanukkah and that reminds me of my mother and that takes me back to the past. But there's something else that I can't quite put my finger on. It's as if this whole struggle I've been having with aging has enabled me to take a look at stuff I couldn't deal with so easily earlier.

"I think I've consolidated something about my Jewish identity that's relatively recent and allows me to think about my own past anti-Semitism in ways I couldn't do comfortably before. When I look inside me now, it's really gone, and I don't think I could truly have said that ever before. Maybe also the distance that comes with age is helping me to think about this stuff now. I was always so ashamed of changing my name and trying to pass that I could barely think about it without wanting to curl up and die. But now that it's so far away, and I feel so solid in so many aspects of my identity, I can look at it all more dispassionately and with a kind of internal quiet I didn't have earlier." I stop speaking and consider my words, then add with a laugh, "Ah, the blessings of age."

Marci walks in. "What's this about the blessings of age? I thought you couldn't see any."

"Just a little irony, dear one. It's a stretch to think about a blessing in getting old, so we take them where we can find them. Actually, I think it's a big step up that I can even consider that getting old may be something other than a curse."

"Way to go, Mom. Pretty soon you may even tell me you like it."

"Don't bet on it."

I go back to tearing up lettuce and recall my anxiety about America's anti-Semites whose voices grew louder and bolder, their diatribes of hate more venomous with each German victory. It can't happen here, I told myself, but it was hard to dismiss people like Father Charles Coughlin, the fiery priest from Detroit, whose weekly radio address was heard by tens of millions of Americans. If his rabid anti-Semitism didn't resonate with something inside those people, why did they listen? From time to time there was also some mob action in which Jews were beaten up, a synagogue burned or defaced, a window broken in a Jewish-owned shop. Each time I heard an anti-Semitic diatribe, each time I read about another swastika painted on a wall in my own city, another attack against innocent Jews, I had visions of *Kristallnacht*—the night in 1938 when the sound of breaking glass filled the air as German hoodlums in uniform wreaked havoc on a sleeping Jewish community, looting more than seven thousand homes and businesses, killing about one hundred, and sending thirty thousand to concentration camps.

Jew! Even now the word on the page seems ominous, filling me with a vague sense of unease, of danger, reminding me of the years when I wanted to hide, to push it away, to flee from the hate that seemed to surround me just because I was a Jew. I can still touch the alarm I felt then when I'd see the word *Jew* scrawled like an epithet on the side of a building. And the self-hatred. *I didn't want to be a Jew!* For no matter how hard we may try to deny its impact, no matter what brave words we use to assure ourselves that we're really okay, maybe even better than "them," it's not possible to live in a world that despises you without turning it in on yourself.

I'm reminded, as I write this, of an exhibit in New York a few years ago called "Too Jewish," its title highlighting the fact that not seeming Jewish, or at least *too* Jewish, has been a central element in American Jewish life. It's true that much has changed in recent generations, that although anti-Semitism isn't gone from the American scene, it's a pale imitation of what I knew in my youth. Yet if the popularity of the exhibition and its reviews are any indication, the sensitivity about seeming too Jewish is alive and well. But what does it mean to be too Jewish?

It means, one of the videos in the show tells us, that when a Jewish girl asks her mother why Jews don't wear the Star of David the way Christians wear the cross, her mother's instant reply is, "Honey, why advertise?" Advice that, especially since the Holocaust, Jews understand in the depth of their being.

It means that Jews change their names more often than others, especially when they're under threat. In the years between 1940 and 1945—the war years—Jews made up 80 percent of the fifty thousand Americans who officially requested permission to change their names.

It means that we distance ourselves from those who are publicly Jewish. Witness our dismay when we see a Hasidic Jew on the streets of our cities.

It means that those of us who don't "look Jewish" feel proud and lucky, and those who do and can afford it spend millions of dollars a year on plastic surgery to remedy the defect. It's true that we now have Barbra Streisand and Minnie Driver, who have abjured plastic surgery—models perhaps of an emerging comfort with looking Jewish. But there's still no dearth of Jewish teenagers who fret because their hair is too curly and their noses too long.

It means that anti-Semitic stereotypes have generated a level of angst and self-hatred that leaves many Jews guarded, wary, and worried about showing themselves as Jews, or, as the show puts it, about being "too Jewish."

Such a response isn't given to Jews alone. It's common among people whose vision of themselves is filtered through the negative stereotypes their society holds up to them—most notably in this country, African-Americans. It isn't simply that blacks and Jews want to look like the beautiful models in the magazines or the handsome movie stars on the screen. Every American probably wants that. The problem is that they internalize the cartoon images of themselves, then seek eagerly for any evidence that they're different. "Good" hair and light skin do it for African-Americans; an upturned nose and a fair complexion for Jews.

I'm aware, of course, that there's another side, the private side of Jewish life where we tell ourselves how much smarter than others we are, where we congratulate ourselves for having produced such a large number of artists and intellectuals, where we revel in our belief that there's something in our culture and our genes that has allowed us to ascend to these heights. But none of that changes the reality that we also organize our lives and public presence around not being too Jewish.

For a little while after I changed my name and declared myself a Protestant, I was fascinated by my new identity. It was seductive to be able to walk around the world as a Christian, to be seen as one of "them," to try to feel my way into the experience. But I soon found myself anxious and troubled. My connection to my family, my ethnic community, my heritage was hidden from the world, had to be hidden if I was to maintain the fiction. When others at work talked about their past, I remained silent. When they asked a question, I made up an answer. "No, my family didn't go to church, so I don't know much about my religion." "Yes, my mother works; she's a saleswoman at Macy's." "My father? He works in a bank." Always occupations that generally weren't open to Jews, and certainly not to immigrant Jews.

Marci interrupts my thoughts again, "I was just thinking about the time you changed your name and pretended not to be Jewish. I mean, it's like gay people who are in the closet and have to listen to straights say things about gays that they'd never say if they knew."

It's striking to me that my daughter has to reach for a modern-

day analogy to grasp the meaning of my experience with anti-
Semitism. It speaks powerfully to the difference in generational
experiences. She feels safe in her Jewishness; I will always be wary
and on guard. "That's a great analogy," I respond, "it's exactly what
it was like. There were lots of times when I had to listen to people
say awful things, like the man in my office who called someone a
'Jew bastard,' or one of the women I worked with who talked contemptuously about 'this kike' who asked her out for coffee, or remarks about Jews taking over the city. They were just part of the
atmosphere in which those people lived. They didn't even think
there was anything wrong with it."

With that Marci and I go off to change out of our grungy jeans
and ready ourselves for our guests, and I'm free once again to return to my thoughts about Christmases and Hanukkahs past.
Then, Hanukkah wasn't talked about in the schools, nor did it
make a dent in Christian America's consciousness anywhere else.
Now, when I turn on TV during the holiday season, it still startles
me to see the menorah on the screen and to hear the announcer
wish me a Happy Hanukkah.

Since no one but Jews thought about Hanukkah then, it
wasn't hard to behave in the larger world as if it wasn't happening. Christmas, however, was another matter. As the holiday approached and people around me talked about their holiday preparations, I had to make up stories that matched theirs. It wasn't long
before my growing inner sense of inauthenticity told me that I
wouldn't be able to sustain the lie much longer.

I wanted to reclaim my name and, with it, the self I had given
away. I'd found out the hard way that a name doesn't just tell the
world who we are, it identifies us to ourselves as well. When I
changed my name something shifted inside me, a distancing that
made me a stranger to myself. All my life I had been, as my mother
said often, "a Breslow." It was a name I bore proudly, even in the
face of her derision. Or perhaps because of it. Now I answered to
a new name and with it a new identity, one I wore with increas-
ing uneasiness.

Each time I had to write my new name, each time I heard it

spoken, I flinched with the knowledge that I had forsaken my birthright and abandoned my people at the very moment when they were being brutalized on the other side of the world. I couldn't get away from shame—ashamed to be a Jew, ashamed not to be. For the other side of Jewish fear and self-hatred is the insistence among Jews that so long as anti-Semitism exists anywhere in the world, we must all stand up and claim our heritage. I was painfully aware that I had violated what for me was the eleventh commandment.

I managed to live with my new identity for about a year before the strain became intolerable. Then I quit my job, took back my name, and with it my self-respect. By then American industry was gearing up to supply the Allied war effort, and the Great Depression was quickly becoming a part of history. As the economy opened up and the need for workers increased, it wasn't so hard for a young Jewish girl to find a job.

My starting salary on my first job was six dollars a week. With some experience and an expanding labor market, I found a job with a weekly wage of ten dollars, an increase that seemed so vast to me I could hardly believe my good fortune. I was hired as a stenographer, but found favor with one of my bosses and soon climbed up to a secretary's desk. Even my mother was impressed.

Years later I was jolted when, in the early days of the feminist movement, I heard my friends and colleagues inveigh against the "shit work" to which secretaries are consigned. Although by then twenty-five years had passed since I worked as a secretary, the rhetoric disturbed me, stirring memories of the pride I felt at being the first in my family to do "clean" work, of the sense of achievement I experienced when I was promoted to the secretarial ranks. I was uncomfortably aware that for many of the women who spent their days at a typewriter, "shit work" was what their mothers had done when they worked in a factory, waited tables in a coffee shop, or cleaned other people's houses.

I tried to rationalize my colleagues' behavior, telling myself that in disparaging the work, they weren't being disdainful of those who did it, that they were motivated by the same desire for justice and equity that lived inside me. I reminded myself that, like them, I also wanted to see more opportunities available to the women who keep the academic, corporate, and professional offices running. But my rationalizations fell victim to resentment. Personally, I was exasperated with people who, having been raised with broad educational and vocational horizons, were unable to grasp the sense of accomplishment possible in the lower-level work that is the lot of most people in any society. Politically, I was troubled about the impact of their elite notions of work and status on the feminist movement.

But I didn't yet know to think any of these things in the years when I went to work each day as a secretary. What I knew then was that I liked my job, did it well, and was rewarded with the respect and approval I couldn't have from the father who died and had never been able to wrest from my mother.

During the day my life seemed light, full, expanding. At night it contracted into the dark and fearful space my mother lived in. In my rational mind I know that, even in the Bronx, people in those days didn't barricade themselves behind the locks and bars that are so common now. Emotionally, however, I carry with me the image of the three of us hunkered down behind bolted doors from which my mother peered out suspiciously when some unlucky person dared to knock.

Yet I continued to live there and turn my paycheck over to her. I grumbled once in a while when the allowance she gave back to me seemed unfair. But I didn't question the basic structure of the arrangement. My class, my culture, and the gender expectations of the community allowed for no other possibilities. Certainly not moving out of my mother's house and finding an independent life. I don't mean I thought of the possibility and rejected it. It simply never occurred to me, or to anyone I knew. Not to a nice Jewish girl.

I knew some women did such things. The switchboard operator in my office was a young single woman who left her home in Iowa and was living alone in New York. I liked Julie and envied her panache, her style, her free spirit, and her blond hair. But she was a *shikseh* and not even a New Yorker. It was impossible for me to identify with her, to look at her life and think that could be me. In the world I lived in, she was categorically written off as a *goyishe nafkeh* (Gentile tramp). As for me, the only way out of my mother's house was to get married, which I did when I was nineteen, the first time an opportunity presented itself.

Marci calls me back from my memories. "Hey, Mom, wake up. What do you want me to do next?" I go back into the kitchen and look around, checking. The chickens are in the oven, the salad is in the frig, the wine and hors d'oeuvres are out, and the *latke* batter, sprinkled with vitamin C to keep it from darkening, is waiting.

"Nothing, it's all done," I reply as I reach out and engulf Marci in a big hug.

"Thanks, I'll take it, but what's that about?" she says, laughing.

I'm not sure; it was a spontaneous moment, something that came from a place inside me that doesn't think. "I don't know," I reply, "maybe just that I'm so happy we're us."

Chapter Nineteen

I sometimes think life is one big accident. I mean you go along thinking that you're living your life consciously, thoughtfully, that you know what you're doing and why. You make decisions, the little ones and the big ones, believing that they'll lead you to a chosen path, only to find that they've taken you to places you never expected to go.

Like going to college. Although I graduated from high school at fifteen, college wasn't an option for me. My task was to get a job as quickly as I could so that, together, my mother and I could help my brother go to college when his turn came. It wasn't that my mother was without aspirations for me; it's just that they didn't include college. "I do dirty work, you'll do clean work" was the mandate with which I grew up. She worked in a factory; I would work in an office. That was more than enough for a girl. "You don't have to go to college; you'll get married, and your husband will take care of you," she declared each time the subject arose.

In truth, my mother's plan for me wasn't so different from my own. I had no objection to her expectation that I would marry well, which meant a professional man who would provide me with all she never could. The difference between us was that I wanted to go to college until that happy day arrived, while for her it was enough that I worked in an office at a nice "clean" job.

Now it seems wholly improbable that, given my mother's own experience, we assumed that some man would enter my life and take care of me forever. But so powerful was the ideology about the roles of men, women, and family life that we took for granted that for me work would be temporary, only until my real life as a wife and mother would begin. Or at most, it would be discretionary, something I would do to keep busy or "help out" should, God forbid, the need arise.

College was reserved for my brother. Never mind that, although he was a year and a half older than I, he was a semester behind me in school. Never mind either that he didn't have much interest in going to college. "How else will he support a family?" my mother demanded when I complained about the inequity of her plans for us. But my protest was a feeble one, born more of sibling rivalry and my anger at the prospect of having to help support my brother through school than of any serious discontent with the gender expectations of the time.

It would be many years before women would make it to my list of the oppressed. I knew that women had a hard road to walk; I had only to look at my mother's life to understand just how cruel the path could be. And long before the issue of college arose, I had already noticed that men always had the better jobs in the factories where my mother worked. Without exception, men were the cutters, the jobs with the highest prestige and the most money. Women worked at the machines, earned less, counted for less.

Since cutting the cloth never seemed to me to require so much more strength or skill than sewing it, I couldn't understand why women weren't cutters, too. My mother, when I asked about it, knew the answer: "Because they're men," she'd retort angrily. But she'd also follow that with the same excuse we still hear today, "They have a family to support." An absurd explanation coming from a woman who had been supporting her family for some years by then. But in the context of the times, it made some sense. My mother simply saw her life as an aberration, an unfortunate deviation from the norm.

Whether in the factory or the office, women simply weren't considered candidates for the higher-status, higher-paying jobs. At least not until the men left for the armed services during World

War II. I'm not saying that men consciously closed women out before that. Or that allowing women entry into the better jobs was something that they, as the gatekeepers, thought about and rejected. It actually was worse than that: They didn't even think about it. Nor did most women. It was as if the gender hierarchy, whether at work or in the family, were given in nature. At home we were wives and mothers, even if we worked. At the office we were typists, secretaries, bookkeepers, file clerks—the helpers men relied on for the background tasks so that they were freed for the important work. "Girls," we were called, as in "Talk to my girl about an appointment." And it didn't occur to most women to object.

I didn't have words like *gender discrimination* to describe what I observed, but I understood that it existed and, in an inchoate and inarticulate way, knew it was unfair. But it didn't seriously occur to me to protest, partly because at the immediate level—the level of my daily life and feelings about it—I was so pleased to be doing what I was doing. It was the clean work my mother had raised me for, and I was proud that I could do it well.

At the deeper psychological level I could ignore my own experience of discrimination in the workplace because it wasn't my gender that seemed so suffocating during the difficult early years of my life. It was the grinding poverty and the struggle to survive; it was living with the fear that my mother would die as suddenly as my father had; it was knowing I couldn't evade my mother's rage and rejection no matter how hard I tried; it was the three of us stuck together in one small room; it was sleeping in the same bed with my mother until I got married. I knew, of course, that my brother had advantages that I didn't; knew, too, that my mother valued him more than me just because he was a son. These things angered me, made me ready to fight, but they didn't sear my soul.

Although I did what was expected, the years never erased from my mind the dream that someday I would get the education that was denied me in my youth. I had been active in left-wing politics all my adult life, from Henry Wallace's campaign for the presidency in 1948 through the McCarthy years, the civil rights movement, the ferment of the 1960s, and into the present. During the two years when I was divorced I made my living managing the congressional campaigns of liberal Democrats in Los Angeles. All I wanted during all those years and the various political actions I engaged in was to be one of the lawyers who took on the civil liberties and civil rights causes with such courage and devotion and who, in doing so, actually made a difference. So when I married Hank and found myself living on the doorstep of the University of California at Berkeley with a husband who was happy to support me both financially and emotionally, it seemed as if my wish could become a reality. I would get my B.A. and go on to law school.

But life had other plans. Instead of becoming a lawyer, I became a sociologist, the result of a chance encounter with one of the professors in the sociology department, where I was taking my undergraduate degree, who saw in me potential I didn't yet know I had.

I entered Berkeley in 1963, long before large numbers of women began returning to college campuses. In my four years as an undergraduate, there was never another grown-up in any of my classes. I was an anomaly, a curiosity whose gray hair (I was still young enough then to leave it alone) stood out among all the blondes, brunettes, and redheads. By the time I was a junior, my advanced age and my academic record had gained the attention of several professors. One of them, concerned that I might not find undergraduate courses stimulating enough, suggested that I try some graduate classes that year. The idea stunned me. In fact, I wasn't bored with most of my undergraduate classes; there was plenty for me to learn.

But I was flattered, intrigued, and exhilarated by the suggestion that my fears about myself were unfounded—that whatever successes I had enjoyed until then weren't simply a matter of luck, looks, timing, or my glib tongue, that I wasn't a sham who would one day be found out. The opportunity to take the next step, to let it take me where it would, became a challenge from which I couldn't retreat.

I didn't think I was giving up the law. Or at least I wouldn't let myself believe it. But by the time I got my B.A., I was halfway to my master's degree, had two articles about to be published, and was totally seduced by the promise of the doctorate. I told myself this was only a detour, that I was enjoying what I was doing and would go to law school after I got my doctorate. But that dream was left for my daughter to fulfill. I had already found too many gratifications in the intellectual life.

It wasn't the last time my life would be thrown off course by a decision I thought was reinforcing a chosen path. I gravitated to sociology as an undergraduate because I wanted a better understanding of the institutional structure of our society in the hope of changing it. But even before I took my first class in college, my political experience had taught me one thing with certainty: One could change institutions overnight if necessary, but the minds and hearts of the people who live in them would not necessarily follow. At the same time, as feminists have learned to their sorrow, a changed consciousness may be a precondition for social change but is no guarantor of it.

So I was frustrated when, at the end of my training, I had learned a great deal about social structure—about institutions and organizations, roles and norms. But I knew little more than I did when I started about the women and men who people the organizations and occupy the roles, which meant also that I still didn't understand the process by which social change could occur.

As I cast around for a way to gain the understanding I sought, I decided that training in clinical psychology would be useful. So as I was finishing my dissertation, I entered a clinical training program. I never expected to practice psychology. I only wanted a deeper understanding of the internal dynamic processes that motivate people, which, I also thought, would help me to a clearer understanding of the subjects of my research and would serve to fine-tune my interviewing skills as well. As before, the route to those goals swerved in expected ways. I got caught up in the clinical experience, no doubt because I was learning at least as much about myself, my childhood, and my relationship with my mother as I was about my patients. It wasn't long before I was seriously training for clinical work and doing the psychological work necessary to do the job well.

As I look back now, I think the decision to become a psychotherapist as well as a sociologist was the single most important one of my entire career. I was awarded my Ph.D. in 1971, when I was forty-seven years old. Even at a much younger age, I would have made an unruly assistant professor; by that advanced age, it would have been impossible for me to fill that role gracefully.

When children can't trust the primary authority figures of childhood, they grow up to an ambivalent and tenuous relationship to authority in adulthood. A psychological reality that was true of me long before I was forty-seven years old. Consequently, I would not have been able to bend easily to the authority of an academic discipline and the treadmill of a tenure track job. The need to publish in the right places, to cultivate the right people, to study the right things in the right way, would surely have pushed every contrary button in my psyche. In becoming a licensed clinician, I was freed to stay out of the university system and still find satisfying professional work and economic independence. Moreover, the practice of psychotherapy being what it is, I was able to limit the number of hours I gave to it each week so that I had time for research and writing, which eventually became the core of my professional identity.

I suppose it's no surprise that thoughts of chance and choice and timing and just plain luck (I'd include God if I were a believer) engage me as my seventy-fifth birthday stares me in the face. I don't quite know what to make of having lived three quarters of a century, how to manage that knowledge, where it fits into the tapestry of my life. But these thoughts are a useful reminder that there are surprises ahead and that any notion I might harbor that I can choose a path and know where it will lead will surely turn out to be a chimera. Not that I really expect to remember the lesson next time I find myself at one of life's choice points.

In my characteristic way, I've fretted and fumed about turning seventy-five, struggling with it for the past year or so, turning it this way and that, trying it on, testing it out, monitoring the fit, as if I could prepare for the reality by anticipating it. It's what sociologists call *anticipatory socialization*. In some ways it worked. Now that the day is almost upon me, it doesn't seem nearly so awesome.

For months friends and family kept asking how I wanted to celebrate this watershed event. Part of me wanted to ignore it, another wanted to mark it in some special way. But nothing I came up with—no great trip abroad, no big bash, no intimate event—seemed right. Finally, Marci announced that she and Diane were planning a party, an event that, I imagined, would be more like the living memorial I once thought I wanted. But I could only surmise, since all they asked of me was the guest list.

"If you don't want to do it, I will. Between Di and me, we pretty well know everyone you'd want to invite," my daughter informed me in a tone that brooked no objection.

I smiled appreciatively, thinking that this must be the way she talks to her subordinates at work, and promised to make up the list. After that they both posted a big "Keep Out" sign on the project.

Until now I've been ambivalent about this party. I'm more than pleased and very moved that my daughter and one of my dearest friends want to do this. When Marci told me about the plan, my thoughts went to my mother, to her curse that my daughter would hurt and disappoint me as I did her, to my gratitude and, yes, triumph that I had foiled her. But my pleasure was mitigated by a distinct uneasiness that I couldn't quite articulate, even to myself. At first it seemed that there was something about being the center of attention that made me uncomfortable. Yet I have enough of the ham in me, enough of a sense of drama, to enjoy center stage, at least for brief moments. So why not now when, in some ways, I've earned it, even if only for having lived so long?

I think about the question as I walk to my clinical office. It's a beautiful morning, crisp and clear, and the walk is invigorating. My office is freezing, as it always is on these winter Monday mornings, which is why I try to get here early enough to get the old-fashioned steam radiator heated up so that my patients and I won't sit shivering through the first hour or two. While I wait for the steam to work its magic, I check the mail, take care of some paperwork I left undone last week, then stand in front of the radiator, warming my back and trying to finish up the morning *Times*, which I brought with me.

But the ambivalence and discomfort I brought into the room seem suddenly to occupy it, so my thoughts return to the question "Why am I uneasy about this party?" As if in answer, the image of the old crone of my dreams rises in my mind. My impulse is to shake my head to try to make her go away, but I've learned by now that her appearance is a signal that my unconscious is trying to tell me something. So I continue to stand quietly in front of the radiator and try to let my mind roam free.

As the minutes pass, my agitation increases until my misgivings rise to something approaching dread. Then without conscious intent I hear my voice saying aloud to the empty room, "I'm ashamed," and with that I know what has kept me from embracing the celebration of my birthday. Not in the normal healthy part of me, but in that dark shadow side that refuses to think, say, or feel the "right" things. In that part I'm ashamed of being old, fearful of being viewed with the same mixture of revulsion and fascination with which I see the old crone of my dreams.

It's not the first time I've felt the shame of getting old, but this feels different, deeper, more centered in my core, and also more appalling, perhaps because I've been struggling with it for so long now. I've always believed that if we know our demons and welcome them into consciousness, they lose the power to run our lives without our consent. So why, after all this time, does this demon retain so much of its charge? I'm irritated with myself and want to shout "Enough! You've been around this track once too many times." Then I remind myself that there's knowing and *knowing*, and that it often takes several laps around the course before we can allow ourselves to know what we know.

I feel impelled now to do something, as if it will help me to know emotionally what, until now, only my head has known. So I pick up the phone, call Marci at her office, and am delighted when her secretary says she can connect me at once. The sound of her voice returns some normalcy to my inner life, but now I feel a little foolish and words escape me for the moment. She listens to the silence for a few seconds, then breaks it. "What's going on? Are you okay?"

"Yeah, I'm fine," I reassure her, "but it's too complicated to explain it all now. It's just that I've been doing my oh-my-God-I'm-about-to-be-seventy-five number for so long, I guess I just needed to touch base to tell you I'm really okay about it, party and all." Before she has a chance to reply, the light signaling my patient's arrival goes on, and we say a quick "love you" and hang up.

I'm pleased to get on with my workday, to leave myself and my thoughts behind as I become absorbed in other people's problems. Most of the time I love this work. Sure, there are moments when I don't want to be in this office, or hours that go so slowly that they try my patience, or even occasionally a person I can't find a way to like and empathize with. But it's almost always intrinsically rewarding, especially for someone who needs to be needed.

I've thought often about this, about how much easier it is for me to be needed than to need, about how much I'd always rather be on the needed side of any interaction. With anyone, that is, except Hank. It's part of what's so special about our bond, the deep and unquestioning knowledge that I can count on him to take care of me, that he will never be driven away by my need.

I have never—*never*—known that about anyone else in my life, not even my daughter, although that's surely not her fault. She has assured me in every way that's humanly possible—and not just with words—that she will always be there, no matter what my need. But what my ears hear and my brain takes in, my heart can't fully comprehend. That hurts Marci, I know, and I wish it weren't so, both for her and for me. But it's one of the costs of my mother's rejection and my father's death that I'll live with for the rest of my life.

Chapter Twenty

With all my accomplishments, the grandest of all, the one that affords me the deepest and most lasting gratification, is having raised this child of mine into the woman she has become. I don't mean to take credit for it all; she certainly did more than her share. And so did luck, a combination of genes and temperament that, unlike my mother and me, made us a good mother–daughter match.

I've often thought how hard it would have been for me to have a child whose mind wasn't as quick as mine. I'm not talking about being smart, just about the speed with which both Marci and I process information, the way we can finish each other's sentences and follow the leaps of mind without having to fill in the blanks. Even Hank, who knows us both so well, sometimes has trouble following our conversations because so much is left unsaid.

Still there were times when it was excruciatingly difficult for me to be the kind of mother I wanted to be. My clinical work, my research, and my own personal experience all have taught me that the psychological theories that claim that childhood psychic trauma are inevitably passed from generation to generation seriously overstate the case. But that doesn't mean it's easy to break the generational chain. And indeed, there were times when my daughter was first born when I wasn't sure I would be able to.

I still shrink from my memories of the months following her birth, from the pain I felt so keenly when I couldn't fulfill the

promise I'd made to myself that I would give my child all the loving kindness I had been denied. I wish I could blame the postpar-
tum illness and the surgery that followed, which incapacitated me
for the first few months of her life. But while I'm certain those
played a part in making the early days of my daughter's life difficult
for me, the deeper problem lay in the psychological injury I
suffered in my own childhood. My infant daughter's utter depen-
dence, the depth of her need, touched my own unmet needs and
found there a well of yearning and resentment I hadn't known
existed.

An image of that time is engraved on my heart: I'm standing at
her crib looking down at her as she sleeps, my heart torn between
love, fear, and resentment. "How can you ask so much when I've
had so little?" I cry silently. "Please don't let me hurt her as I've
been hurt," I beg a God I don't believe in.

I know I'm not alone in this struggle. I've heard this story
many times, both in my clinical work and in my research. I'm reminded of Ana Guittierez, one of the women I wrote about in *The
Transcendent Child*. The daughter of a migrant farm family, Ana es-
caped a violent father, an ineffective mother, an abusive husband,
and the fields in which she toiled from childhood until she was in
her early twenties. When I met her, she was completing a doctoral
program in child psychology and development. As a child she
dreamed about flying away to another family; as an adult she
vowed that she would be the kind of parent she longed for but
didn't have. "From the time I got pregnant, I had a plan in place; I
was going to be a really caring, loving, nurturing parent, different
than they were to me."

But for people who have been inadequately nurtured in their
own childhood, there's often a gap between their wishes and what
they're able to do for their children. So there were times, particularly when her baby was sick and needy, when Ana simply couldn't
be there as fully as her child needed. "I couldn't help it; I didn't
have it to give, and I disengaged. How I wish there was a way to do
it over again."

What parent doesn't know the wish "to do it over again," to

have a second chance, to correct the mistakes of the past? For me, it was particularly affecting to listen to Ana's regrets, for they so closely mirrored my own. It isn't that I was a bad mother, any more than Ana was. Like her, I steeled myself to do what had to be done. And most of the time I pulled it off with no one but me the wiser. But like Ana, I'll never fully forgive myself for being unable, in those first months of my daughter's life, to mother her with the generosity of spirit my child deserved.

Years later, when Marci entered therapy to help her get out of a bad marriage and we reminisced about the issues of the past that might have led her there, I thought it might be helpful for her to know about my maternal lapses during the first year of her life. (I didn't have to tell her about all the fumbles and stumbles that followed; those she could remember.) Being a therapist's child, she knew better than to shrug and say, "So what; I don't remember that." Instead she hugged me and said, "Yeah, Mom, I've always known you weren't perfect, but somehow I managed to survive it."

The phone rings. It's my unlisted line, which, since only friends and family have that number, means there's someone at the other end I ordinarily would want to speak with. But I'm so engaged in my thoughts that I let the machine pick it up until I hear Marci's voice, "Hey, where are you? I thought you'd be there since I know this is a writing day."

I pick up the call. "If I believed in psychic communication, I'd think this is one of those moments. I've just been writing about you."

"Good, you can tell me about it at lunch at Lulu's if you can tear yourself away," she says, knowing how hard it is for me to walk away from my computer on these days. It doesn't matter whether the writing is going well or badly; either way I'm chained to it psychologically as surely as if I were bound by steel. If the writing is flowing easily, I can't bear to stop; if I'm staring at the screen without a clue to what the next sentence will be, it's equally hard to leave before I can find the thought and put it into words.

Right now, however, I'm surprised at her invitation to lunch.

She has been so busy that I haven't seen her for weeks and lunch in the middle of the workday, even when she's in town, has been out of the question. "Everything okay?" I ask in my reflexive mother style.

She laughs; it's a joke between us. As she tells it, I phone her, she says hello, and I say, "What's the matter?" In truth, it goes both ways; she's as acutely sensitive to my moods as I am to hers, and she knows instantly from the tone of my voice on the phone if something isn't well with me. For both of us, that kind of near telepathy can be both a blessing and a curse, as Marci would be the first to say. It's wonderful to feel known and understood like that, but it can also be intrusive, leaving too little room for the privacy of thought and feeling. Now she says, "Everything's fine; I just decided I need some time away from this place, and it's been too long since the last time we did this."

What mother can resist those words from an adult child?

The sun peeked out briefly earlier this morning, but by the time I leave for the three-mile walk to the restaurant, a cold fog has moved in through the Gate, and the wind that whips off the bay stings my cheeks, makes my nose run, and blows my short hair into a trendy mess. It's good to be out, away from the writer's cave I'm immersed in so much of the time these days, away from my love-hate relationship with the process.

Love-hate relationship? The words rattle around in my brain while I ask myself if I really mean it. I don't, at least not the hate part. But I certainly have a complicated relationship to this work I do, as I believe all writers must. I love the *process* of writing, even when it hurts. It can be painful, frustrating, isolating, and agonizingly difficult. But when it works at its best—when the creative process takes hold and I find myself with thoughts I didn't know I had, when the words and ideas flow from some place inside me that seems to be out of my control—the exhilaration I feel, the mystical and magical quality of the experience, is like nothing else in life, except perhaps birthing a child.

But there's a cost, and therein lies my ambivalence. For I'm caught between loving the gratification of doing something that engages me so deeply and resenting that, when I'm in that place, everything else—other work I value, an evening out with friends, lunch and a walk with my husband, a concert, the ballet—all feel like an unwelcome interruption. Not, however, lunch with my daughter.

My walk takes me down the face of Nob Hill and through Chinatown with its hundreds of restaurants where exquisitely bronzed ducks and slabs of spareribs hang in the windows. My mouth waters as I pass one of the many dim sum emporiums and the odor of those tasty morsels wafts through the air.

After years of ambling through this neighborhood, I'm still captivated by its sights and sounds—by the tanks of live fish packed so tightly that they keep bumping up against the dirty glass, by the food stalls that spill onto the sidewalks and the trucks of live poultry that line the streets, by the little old Chinese house-wives who elbow you out of their way to get just the eggplant or bok choy they have their eye on, by the shoppers and lookers and tourists, all caught up in the incredible energy of this vibrant com-munity that looks, feels, and tastes as if it belongs to another era.

I stop for a light, and by the time it turns green, my way across the street is blocked by a Chinese funeral procession, complete with huge poster-sized photographs of the deceased and a sad col-lection of musicians whose main function seems to be to make enough noise to alert the ancestors that one of their own is com-ing. I smile as I watch them pass, thinking how much I love this city—its neighborhoods, each with its own ambience, its own moods; its tolerance, even encouragement of differences.

I'm not naive about this. I know there are ethnic and racial tensions here, that as our Asian population has grown to more than one third of the city and Latinos to nearly one fifth, many white folks are uncomfortable about having become a minority in the city they always thought belonged to them. Nevertheless, we live relatively well together here compared to many other places in the country.

As I walk and watch, I'm also thinking about my daughter, about how different our relationship is from the one I had with my mother, about how much we have shared. Even a three-week stint in jail. It was the fall of 1967, at the height of the student protests against the Vietnam War. I was a forty-three-year-old graduate student at Berkeley; Marci was a nineteen-year-old undergraduate. We were both active in the political struggles on campus, sometimes in the same sphere, sometimes in our separate ones. We walked the picket lines, faced the police with their nightsticks and gas masks, ran with burning eyes from the tear gas they sprayed at us. As the Christmas break approached, the leaders of the antiwar movement planned a demonstration at the Oakland Induction Center.

Hank and I both opposed the Vietnam War strongly; we both wanted to do our part in making a public statement of our opposition. But we were also fearful about being in jail at the same time. It seemed prudent that one of us should stay out to provide help and legal services if they were needed. Little did we know how much that would be the case.

We decided I should be the one to join the protest, partly because he was running a couple of businesses at the time and I was only a student; partly because his contacts and reputation in the Berkeley community, where he had been active professionally and politically for many years, gave him a wide reach should we need it; and partly also because I couldn't bear the thought of one day looking back on this historical moment and wondering what I was doing and why my voice wasn't heard.

When next I talked with Marci I told her about our decision. "That's great, Mom, I've been wondering how to tell you that I was planning to go and get arrested. Now we can go to jail together."

We laughed, but I was frightened. When it was just me, I could tell myself it wouldn't be so bad, that it would only be for a couple of days, that I've lived through worse. But my child in jail! That was another thing. The only comfort I could take from the thought was that we'd be there together.

At five o'clock on the morning of December 16, 1967, my daughter and I, along with sixty-seven other women and about one hundred men sat down in front of the buses that were carrying the young men who had been drafted to the induction center. As the buses approached each line of protesters, the police swept us into wagons that carried us off to jail, some to Oakland, others to the county jail in Santa Rita.

No matter how long I live, I'll never forget the moment I watched them take my daughter away, or the terror I felt when, a short while later, I was locked into a cell at the Oakland city jail and had no idea where she was. Until that moment I had never seriously imagined what going to jail would mean. The night before the demonstration a friend, who is a criminal attorney, tried to talk me out of going to it. "Are you sure you want to do this?" he asked. "Do you have any idea what it's like being locked up in a six-by-six-foot cell?"

In my ignorance, I waved away his concerns with cavalier reassurances. It was easy to get caught up in the cause, in the romance of the demonstration, in the excitement of being a part of something larger than myself, in the adrenaline rush that comes with toying with danger. But when the reality hit and I was suddenly facing the finality of the barred door clanging shut, I would have given anything to be anywhere else. I was certain, in that instant, that I was about to choke on the panic that welled up inside me and closed off my breath. My cell mate, an old hand at jail time, watched me with disgust for a moment or two, then thrust her menacing face into mine and spat out the words, "One of those goddamn Commie protesters, huh? Jesus, what did I do to deserve you in here?"

I didn't see Marci again until we were brought to court the next morning, where we pleaded no contest and were stunned to be sentenced to three weeks in the county jail at Santa Rita. Elsewhere in the country protesters were given one- or two-day sentences, sometimes even released after being held for only a couple of hours. But this was California. Ronald Reagan was our governor and the judge was one of his first judicial appointees. They made it clear that they wanted to teach us, and whoever might come after, a lesson.

Talk about a bonding experience. My daughter and I slept in a dormitory with sixty-seven other women, our cots so close together that we sometimes fell asleep clutching each other's hands. We laughed at the same things, tried not to cry about the same things, suffered the same indignities, read the same books, dreamed about what we'd do when we got out, organized a sit-in together when the prison administration treated our group with undue harshness. As difficult as those three weeks were, they were far more tolerable than they would otherwise have been because we had each other.

We still sometimes talk about those weeks in jail, recalling both the anger and the laughter, and especially the moment when we were in the food line and one of the servers, a long-term criminal (as opposed to political) inmate, looked us up and down and said to Marci, "Hey, girl, I heard that's yo' mama; that true?"

Marci, proud to be there with me, answered, "Yeah, that's my mom."

The woman shook her head in bewilderment. "Damn, now I seen everything. You must be crazy, girl; it's bad enough to be in this stinking place, but to bring yo' mama . . ." Her words trailed off as if unable to express the inexpressible.

Her response, however, wasn't so different from my family's. When my mother heard that Marci had been to jail with me, she was furious. "How could you let her do that?" she demanded as if I could have stopped her even if I had wanted to. "She's a ruined woman now," she declared. "Who will want a jailbird?"

A few months later, when my brother came to visit, he took me aside one evening after Marci had dinner with us, "I don't know how you could have let that beautiful girl go to jail. What decent man will marry her now?" It was beyond his understanding, even when I tried to explain, that in the world Marci lived in she had become more desirable, not less, for having, as we said in those days, "put her body on the line."

I've been so engrossed in my thoughts that I didn't notice when I left Chinatown behind me and turned onto Kearny Street, a low-rent area at the edge of downtown with an assortment of downscale shops that can't afford the rents of the trendier spots just a block or two away. It's a neighborhood with no name, which is somehow appropriate, given its nondescript mien. It strikes me, as I look around, that places like this become a self-fulfilling prophecy. The stores here can't support the rents in the heart of the city, so they set up unattractive little shops a few blocks away, which don't appeal to the shoppers with money, thereby practically guaranteeing that the best they can hope for is enough business to stay where they are.

After I cross Market Street, with its old-fashioned electric trolleys that chug across the city from the bay to the famous Castro district, I come upon Yerba Buena, a recently gentrified neighborhood—changed from the site of run-down apartments, decrepit hotels, and seedy businesses to a smart complex of theaters, gardens, the beautiful new San Francisco Museum of Modern Art, and the Convention Center with a marvelous Children's Center next door, which boasts a turn-of-the-century merry-go-round on one of the city's busiest corners.

I'm cold and windblown, but exhilarated by my walk and happy to sit and sip tea while waiting for Marci to arrive. I think of what I'm writing about her and wonder if I'm making our relationship seem too idyllic, a kind of mother-daughter perfection that's more a fantasy than a reality. In fact, neither of us is an easy person. We're both impatient, opinionated, somewhat volatile, tend to irritability, don't suffer fools easily, and expect a lot of ourselves and others. The doctoral students I've supervised would be the first to tell you that I asked more of them than they thought they could do. Which for some was the gift of a lifetime, for others a greater burden than they chose to carry. I see Marci doing the same thing with the men and women who work for her.

Two such strong personalities are bound to clash from time to time. I was a loving mother, even an adoring one at times, but not an easy one. And like all teenagers and young adults she found creative ways to affirm her separateness and assert her independence—ways I sometimes found hard to take, like joining a sorority in high school, or leaving law school in the middle of her last year to go skiing. What better way to separate from a determinedly egalitarian mother whose lifetime wish was to go to law school?

If my expectations for my students were high, imagine what they were for my daughter—not about what she would do, but that she would do something. And do it well. Going to college, becoming a professional woman—these were aspirations fed to her with her mother's milk. As were the political and social values to which I've devoted my adult life. One of her earliest memories, she says, is sitting in some campaign office and pasting address labels on flyers advocating for some cause or candidate. Perhaps not the ideal entertainment for a three-year-old, but the beginning of the lessons in social responsibility she carries with her to this day.

It isn't that we talked all the time about her future or about our beliefs and values, maybe not even much of the time. It was mostly just there, in the air, as much a part of life as eating and sleeping. And so was the intensity of our bond, even when she was struggling the hardest to find her own identity and push my voice out of her head. We had our moments then, not the kind of baleful and bitter conflict I see in other families, but a more subtle form, a pulling away, a way she had of distancing herself, of leaving without leaving, that was hard for me.

I'd tell myself during those times that she needed to separate, that it was better for both of us, that I needed to be patient with her, that I should take comfort in the knowledge that she seemed always to keep one foot in the values of our family. But it wasn't easy, and there were many moments when she tested my faith. How could I know what the outcome would be when, during her freshman year at college, she was, in the language of the day, tuning in, turning on, and threatening to drop out?

I don't know what Marci would say about those times (although I'll surely find out when she reads these words) but as I see it, what got us through even the worst of times was a deep and abiding respect for each other and a profound trust in the relationship itself that never wavered—not then, not now. We still get irritated with each other and roll our eyes at some characteristic behavior we would wish away if we could, but the bonds of love and respect make it easy to transcend these momentary annoyances and appreciate what we have together.

I look at my watch; she's late and it's unlike her. As always in a moment like this, my anxiety rises: Is this the right time? Am I in the right place? Annoyed with myself, I signal the waiter to refill my tea and return to my musings. An image of Marci as a child comes up from my memory bank and reminds me how different that little girl was from the woman I know now. She was a shy, quiet child who was uneasy in the world of her peers and whose second grade teacher worried that her "intellectual skills were advanced beyond her social skills." I never could figure out what that teacher wanted me to do about that. It's one thing to ask a parent to help a child with reading or arithmetic, but with social skills? Are we supposed to try to remake our children to fit some popular image of what they ought to be?

As she got older her social skills caught up and I could stop worrying about what to say to her teachers at conference time. But she was never one of the "in" kids at any time during her school career, from elementary school right through high school. Indeed, it was impossible then to imagine that she'd grow up to be the outgoing, dynamic woman she has become.

I look up to see my daughter rushing toward me with a smile and an apology for being late. She has just come back from a business trip and although she's bouncy and happy, she looks tired. I watch her settle herself across the table as my mind flashes on some of the difficult moments in our shared lives—my separation from her birth father when she was twelve; the two years after my divorce when I was so intensely consumed by my work as a political campaign manager that there was little time or energy for anything else; my marriage to Hank and our move from Los Angeles to Berkeley, which didn't please her at all; her troubled relationship with her birth father who, soon after we left Los Angeles, gave her up to Hank for adoption.

Why am I thinking about the hard things now? Perhaps I need the reminder that she has survived a lot more than my imperfect mothering, and that not all of it was in my control. Or maybe it's to underscore the point that, in human development, the line from the present to the future often takes unpredictable twists and turns.

I can't help feeling the glow of pride as I see her sitting before me, a hugely successful woman in both her personal and professional life who is also my little girl. I smile at the maternal narcissism and identification that underlies my pride, as if I deserve some credit for her accomplishments. I suppose it's inevitable for a parent to feel some of that, although it makes me mildly uncomfortable, so I rush to remind myself that she didn't need a lot from me to find success, at least not in the world of work.

She was always a quick study. In high school she could do her homework while watching TV and talking on the phone, and still get an A. In law school she waltzed through, opening her books only in time to take the exams. Given that past, I wonder sometimes what motivated the drive necessary for such a successful career.

My friend Dorothy, who has known her since she was a child, says it's no surprise. "She doesn't know how *not* to do things well. When she decided she was going to be a hippie, she was at the top the class. It was the same when she was waiting tables. So once she decided she would actually be a lawyer, I never had any doubt that she'd be great at it."

Marci has another answer when I've asked the question. "What else could I do with you for a mother? Maybe I didn't always like it, but I always knew I had to do well. You expected a lot, Mom; not that you said it; I just knew. It was one thing to spend a few years fooling around—dropping out of law school for a couple of years, then working as a cocktail waitress instead of taking the bar after I finally graduated. But once I decided take the bar and be a lawyer, I couldn't do anything but my best."

Now that she's done it, she has been talking about leaving her job for some time, and we pick up that conversation again. As deputy general counsel for a national corporation she has achieved a level of status and prestige that makes her, in her words, "a player" in that world. "It's not easy to give all that up," she says. "I'll leave a lot on the table besides money if I leave next year, but that will be true no matter when I go. There'll always be a reason not to go—another challenge, another raise that's more than most people make in a year, more stock options that will take years to vest.

"I've been saying for a year now that I want to be out of there by the time I'm fifty. Well, I didn't make it; I'm fifty and still here. Now with the merger, I've agreed to one more year to get the department through it, then I want to be gone. I don't want work to take up so much of my life anymore; I have too many other things I want to do."

"I worry sometimes that you haven't taken seriously enough what it will feel like to leave those things behind," I say. "Not the money, the other perks."

"I know you do, and I wonder sometimes whether you're thinking about me or you. I mean, I know how proud you are of me, and maybe you have trouble thinking about me giving up my job because it's important to you to have me in this position."

Her remark stings. I want to object, but I hold my tongue while my thoughts go at once to my mother who never acknowledged my accomplishments to me but used them to enhance herself in the eyes of others. Is this what my daughter thinks of me? I reassure myself: It's different, she knows how proud I am of her; she just said so. Still the question touches a nerve, perhaps because it forces me to confront the kernel of truth in what she says.

"It's a hard question," I finally say, "and I've been thinking of how to respond. It's certainly true that I'm very proud of your success, and I'm sure it's important to me. Since moms get blamed for anything that goes wrong with their kids—and I've worried plenty about all the things I did wrong—I figure I'm entitled to take some credit when it goes right. But it's not just your professional success that I take pleasure in. I think what I'm most proud of is who you are and how you've taken the political and social values you were brought up with into this huge corporation and made a difference."

She smiles almost shyly. "I love hearing you say those things, and I also know that you're right that it won't be easy to give this position up. Right now people answer the phone when I call because of my title, not because I'm Marci Rubin. I like that, being somebody, and it wouldn't be easy to go back to being nobody."

She continues talking but I miss the rest of her words because the last phrase makes me feel as if I've been kicked in the stomach. This is exactly what I've been feeling as I've watched old age creep up, that I've gone back "to being nobody." "Yes," I say when I can catch my breath again, "I know what that feels like, and I don't want you to suffer it."

She rolls her eyes, as if she can't believe what she's just heard. "Don't tell me you feel like a nobody, Mom; that's nuts. I don't know how you can say that; I think this birthday is making you soft in the head. Your public presence is attached to your work, mine is attached to my job. People know what you do. With me no one outside the company knows what I actually do. I'm a player out there only because of the position I hold. When I say that I have several hundred "friends" who won't know me the day I quit my job, I'm talking truth. That's absolutely untrue for you; people will know and respect what you've written—which, let's face it, is also a lot who you are—long after you're gone."

Maybe that's true, but it's equally true that my professional life is quieter these days than it has ever been. Where before I felt in high demand, now my phone rings much less often with requests for a lecture, an interview, a profile, some words of wisdom or a sound bite about an event in the world. My head tells me this probably has nothing to do with my age, but in my heart I wonder, "Is it just a coincidence that the silence comes at this time in my life? Or is there some perception out there that my time has passed, that what I have to say is no longer as interesting, important, or relevant as it once was?"

This is one of the most difficult things about getting old, this sense that you're no longer in the mainstream of life. My friend Riese, who's about to be sixty-five, says there are some aspects of aging that feel easier than she'd anticipated. "Instead of feeling pressed for time now that I understand so clearly how finite it is, I feel more at ease with time. I'm less impatient with myself and less in conflict, and the tyranny of work, of always being productive, seems to have loosened its hold somewhat."

What troubles her most deeply, however, is her fear of becoming irrelevant, of finding herself devalued and peripheral in a world where once she was center stage. "I can't tolerate the idea that I won't count in the world, or that what I can contribute won't continue to be welcomed. It seems ironic that I have to leave the scene when, for the first time in my life, I actually feel like a wise person at times. The thought that I won't be valued and my contributions won't be recognized frightens and depresses me most of all."

Marci and I finish lunch, and I walk with her back to her office, which is just a block away. We hug warmly as we say good-bye, and she holds on for an extra moment, as if afraid I might disappear if she lets go. I hold her tightly and say, "Not to worry; I'm not going anywhere for a while."

"I know, but I worry about you," she says, and, with one last squeeze, turns and disappears into the building, swallowed up not just by the brick and mortar but by the busy life she lives inside there.

I know I should get back to work, but I need time to think, so I forgo the taxi that cruises by and decide to walk the mile or so to the bus stop. On my way I think about how different Marci's response is to my aging and impending death than mine was with my mother. For me whatever pain existed was related to the failure of the relationship; for her it's connected to its success. Where I saw my mother's old age as a burden that I had to be involved in, my daughter clearly wants to share these years fully.

It's true, of course, that I'm not old in the same way my mother was old, nor am I likely to be the burden she was for many more years. Never, I hope, if I can keep my promise to myself to die when I know the time is right. Still, I'm surprised sometimes when I see the subtle ways our relationship has changed since my mother's death, as if the realization that I now stand at the head of the generational line makes the possibility of my death more concrete to her. Or perhaps it's simply the fact that I'm turning seventy-five so soon after I had a brush with death. Or perhaps it's all of the above and something more that I know nothing about. Whatever the reason, there's a heightened concern about me, whether about my feelings or my health, and a new and deeper tenderness that I haven't seen before.

I see it happening in other families as well. As their awareness of the limits of time has grown—partly because of their parents' aging, partly because of their own passing years—younger friends whose parents live in distant cities visit them more often now than they used to. Older friends, those in their sixties and seventies, tell me that their children have grown more attentive, that they phone more often and invite their visits more urgently.

For Marci, the combination of her own fiftieth birthday coming just six months before my seventy-fifth (and not to be forgotten, Hank's impending eighty-third) has brought a new awareness of aging and mortality, both hers and ours, and with it a kind of poignancy to the attachment that makes itself felt in those moments of holding on, in her discomfort about being out of touch for any length of time, in her expressions of concerns about our health, in her desire to spend more time with us, as if she can store us up now for the time when we won't be around.

My eyes tear, this time not from the wind. There's an ache deep inside me, a pain that grows with every step. I never imagined I could feel it but I envy my daughter. Envy her for the mother she has, for her unwavering certainty about her mother's love, for the real tears she will shed when her mother dies, for the welcome images that will live inside to warm her when that time comes.

I envy her all that while I also know that I've given myself a gift at least as large as the one I gave her. Against all odds, I fulfilled my promise; I've broken the generational chain. It's the great victory of my life. It has been a healing, gratifying, and triumphant journey to become for my daughter the mother I wanted my mother to be for me.

Chapter Twenty-one

It's Friday, the day before my birthday party, which, for the moment, has taken over my life. Friends are arriving from other places and we want to welcome them, so Hank and I spent part of yesterday and all morning today cooking for the dinner we'll have at home tonight. We're good cooks, both of us, but have little interest now in doing the kind of simple meals we prepare daily. So we're always happy to exercise our culinary skills and prepare the more elaborate meals we serve to others.

After three hours in the kitchen, it's time to take a break. Hank goes off to do some errands; I get ready to meet my friend Gail for lunch. When we arranged this date some weeks ago, she thought perhaps we ought to do something different, a special treat for this special moment. But the more I thought about it, the less the idea appealed to me. It seemed as if there was already too much specialness about this birthday; I didn't need anymore. Instead I wanted to honor the continuities in my life, the familiar, the habitual, the commonplace, the everyday activities that would allow me to believe I could count on them into the uncertain future that lies ahead.

"Why don't we do what we always do," I suggested, meaning that we'd meet at a restaurant on Union Street, where we go to share a great chicken sandwich.

Everyplace is downhill from where I live, so when I leave my apartment building I turn the corner and head down the four steep blocks to Polk Street, which, before the Castro gained favor, used to be the center of San Francisco's homosexual community. Now Polk is just the street that stretches across the western foot of both Nob and Russian Hills, one of those urban streets that's lined with the kind of shops and services that cater to any neighborhood's needs—dozens of coffee shops for a city that never stops drinking coffee, restaurants (what is a street in San Francisco without a couple of dozen restaurants?), an upscale takeout deli and several lower down on the status chain, food markets, greengrocers, bookstores, photo shops, card shops, jewelers, pharmacies, dry cleaners, and the ever present Gap and Radio Shack.

A mile or so later, I come to Union Street and walk through Cow Hollow, a name that, the city's historians say, is a remnant of the days when cows roamed this little hollow nestled between San Francisco's famous Russian Hill and its tony Pacific Heights. It's hard now to think of cows here, but often when I walk through this neighborhood, my mind wanders to that earlier time and tries to imagine what it was like without the endless boutiques and restaurants that now line the street from one end of the hollow to the other. It's a lovely, bucolic vision, quite at odds with the restless energy and urban noise that now dominate the atmosphere here.

Gail is waiting for me when I arrive and has already ordered. We greet each other with a hug, then she sits back and surveys me carefully before asking, "So, what's it like?"

I don't have to ask what she means; I know. But I've had enough of thinking about this birthday, more than enough of talking about it. "Do we have to?" I ask, sounding somewhat churlish.

"No, not if you don't want to," she says quietly.

But the subject lies between us like the proverbial elephant in the middle of the room. I sigh, "I guess I can't get away from it, can I? It isn't that I mind talking about it; it's just that I don't have anything new to say. And I think I get a little uptight when that seems to be all everyone wants to talk about, as if this damn birthday defines who I am."

"Well, my dear friend," she says, her eyes smiling but her manner serious, "I think it's you who are doing that, not your friends. I certainly don't think being seventy-five is who you are, but you've been acting as if you think so. So, of course, we're concerned."

I know she's right. "Yes, I know," I reply, feeling chastened. "I've been struggling with how to get old since my mother died, and it's as if this birthday is the climax of these last couple of years. It's a milestone I have to get past, then maybe I'll be able to tell both of us what it's like."

The conversation moves easily to other things—her husband, a psychologist who has developed into a fine artist in recent years, her eight-year-old daughter, my writing, our clinical work. It's not unusual for us to share a case, one of us working with the individual, the other with the couple, and when we have our patients' permission, an exchange of information and perspectives is useful for them and for us.

She has to get back to work, I to the kitchen. I walk the few blocks to her office with her, then hail a cab. At home, Hank has set the table and is at his desk putting the finishing touches on an article about food and wine that's due for publication sometime in the next few months. He looks up with a smile when I enter the room. "How's Gail?" he asks.

I can't answer because I'm suddenly choked with emotion— love, joy, sorrow, all of it welling up at once as my heart fills with this man I've lived with for so long and who I now keep preparing myself to lose. I try to shake off the fear that grips me, reaching for thought instead of feeling, "Is it that I'm afraid to lose him, or is it my own life that seems so fragile now?" It doesn't feel that way. But perhaps when it come to my own death, the denial mechanisms that don't work so well elsewhere drop easily into place.

I put my arms around him and say teasingly, "I swear I'll never talk to you again if you die and leave me; you hear?"

He holds me tightly, my head buried against his chest. I can't see his face but I know, as well as I know anything in this life, the expression of love and tenderness he wears. We move apart, smiling through the sadness that fills the room, "I couldn't stand your not talking to me, so I won't die, I promise," he says, completing his half of the little playlet we act out from time to time. We laugh then with genuine mirth, joyful at the fullness of our life, our love, at the silliness that gets us through these moments when the spotlight in our minds illuminates the daunting reality ahead.

The only thing left to do for dinner is dessert. Baking is my territory, with Hank playing the role of kitchen helper. Tonight it will be a warm chocolate cake, which I can prepare in advance and bake just before it's served with the vanilla ice cream I made this morning.

It's seven o'clock, our guests will arrive momentarily. Meanwhile we sip a glass of wine and look out over the city, its lights illuminating the fog bank that lies just outside the Gate while closer in they twinkle and sparkle with a brilliance that prompts me to say, "It looks as if God shined up the world out there, doesn't it?"

I'm aware, as I speak, that for someone who's a nonbeliever, I seem to invoke God a lot. Usually I think of it as a joke, a way of expressing my awe at something beautiful, or even something mundane. Sometimes when we're trying to make a choice between this restaurant or that, between this movie or that, I'll see a parking space and quip, "That settles it; God wants us to go here." Now I ask myself if this is a remnant from a past when my mother called upon God with an endless series of requests he never seemed to hear, or at least didn't attend to.

As a child I never understood the nature of my mother's belief, although she proclaimed it loudly and often, beseeching God with a steady stream of requests. I have no doubt that she was a believer and found some comfort in her belief, but her connection to both her religion and her faith always seemed so hypocritical to me, so self-serving, so without the reverence and devotion I think of when I contemplate the truly religious. So when I was eight years old, I decided to test the faith—and my already wobbly belief in God—empirically.

It was Yom Kippur, the holiest day in the Jewish calendar, a day for fasting and repentance. Although my mother went to synagogue only to observe *Yiskur* (the memorial prayer for the dead), which came at the end of the day's service and was free, she always fasted through the day, and my brother and I were expected to do the same—not an easy feat for a small child. Inside the house it was even more somber than usual—no light permitted, the kitchen closed for the day, the *yurtseit* (memorial) candle for my father flickering on the oilcloth-covered table. Outside, it was one of those warm Indian summer days in New York that almost always appear around the Jewish holidays. All I wanted was to get out into it and distract myself from my grumbling stomach.

The Bronx neighborhood where I lived was completely closed down on this day—the shops dark, the usually bustling street life stilled for the moment. As I wandered around the quiet streets, I kept getting farther and farther from home until I found myself in an Italian neighborhood that was fully alive—children running around while their mothers did their marketing, the bins on the street overflowing with a mouth-watering array of food. I walked up and down looking at the food hungrily, wishing I had money to buy a candy bar, an apple, anything to appease the growing hunger inside me. Finally, the temptations were too much. I stole a candy bar—a Milky Way—and, my heart beating wildly, ran off to find a place where I could eat it safely.

I can still feel the warmth of the sun on my face as I stood on that street corner in the Bronx holding the candy bar in my hand. I had already committed one sin when I stole the candy. Would I dare commit the second, and what seemed to me the far worse one, and eat it? What if there was a God; what would he do to me? I smile as I write these words and think, "Was this what Adam worried about when he took that bite of the apple?"

Finally, the candy won over conscience. I ate greedily, all the while looking up at the sky and waiting for some presence up there to strike me down. But it was only my mother who, when I came home, took one look at my guilty face and beat me up. I suppose a believer would say that God's punishment was delivered through my mother's hands. But to me it was just another day at home with Mother.

It would be easy to blame my profound religious disaffection on what seemed to me to be my mother's hollow relationship to religious belief. And there may be some truth in that. But there are larger issues. We believe in God because we need some way to explain life's uncertainties, some sense that there's an order, an explanation for the unexplainable. But he never seemed to explain anything to me—not then, not now.

I couldn't, even as a child, trust a God who would allow the anger and cruelty I knew inside my home and the barbarity I saw outside, as Adolf Hitler ordered the murder of six million Jews, millions of gypsies and homosexuals, and an assortment of others he deemed unworthy of life. As soon as I was old enough to think my own thoughts, therefore, I reached for the rational and secular explanations to life's conundrums. They, at least, didn't promise anything they couldn't deliver, didn't ask me to suspend disbelief in the hope of some reward or understanding that would never come.

The bell interrupts my thoughts as our guests arrive. It's wonderful to see these friends who have come from faraway places to celebrate this time with us. Hank opens a bottle of Veuve Cliquot, a fine French champagne, and we toast to our friendship, to the wonderful times we've shared, to our hopes for a long future together. "At least theirs will be long," I think as I survey my friends who are anywhere from ten to thirty years younger than I am.

It's a perfect evening—the food, the wine, the guests, the conversation—one of those moments you want to hold on to, so although I'm tired, I'm sorry to see it end. After the rush of goodbye hugs, we finish the cleanup, turn off the lights, and head for bed. But I'm too keyed up to sleep, so I read for a while while Hank turns off the light on his side of the bed and falls instantly asleep. Finally, fatigue closes in, and I put the book away, turn out the light, and fall into a light, restless slumber. I'm not surprised, even in my dream, when the old crone pays me another visit.

I'm walking in a lovely garden, not one of those neatly manicured ones but a garden that's relaxed and informal, as if designed by nature instead of the human hand. There's a path at the far end of the garden and I wander over, wondering where it will lead me. As I approach it, I see the old crone standing off to one side, a daffodil in her hand. I know she's the same person, but she no longer looks like the woman I met earlier. Her hair has been stylishly cut and her long skirt and tunic are something I might wear. I start to go by, expecting her to block my path, as she has in the past, but she just hands me the flower she's holding, then steps away and lets me pass.

Half-awake, I lie there, trying to hold on to the dream, to fix it in my mind. "Maybe this won't be so bad after all," I think, as I sink back into sleep.

When I wake again in the morning, I'm pleased that the day has finally arrived, but I can't tell whether that's because I'm happy about it or I'm just glad to know it will soon be over. This birthday has consumed too much of my mental and emotional energy, and right now I resent it. It's hard to settle down to anything—not work, not reading a book, not phoning a friend, not going for a walk—so I go to the gym (what better way to say fuck you to seventy-five?) and work out strenuously for an hour or so. When I come back, I spend another couple of hours baking cookies, another task I can count on to provide an easy and pleasant distraction.

When it's finally time to get dressed, I stand in my closet surveying more clothes than anyone has a right to own, and try to decide what I'll wear. I'm not proud of the extravagant display. I understand that my unruly appetite for clothes is a direct response to the fact that as a child I had only the clothing my mother sewed for me, clothes that were always waiting for me to grow into them. But I also know that even when the heart understands what the brain knows, we can't always bind the wounds with rational behavior.

I know I'm anxious when I try on three or four different outfits before settling on a black silk pant suit with a velvet mandarin collar trimming its Chinese-style jacket and a white satin tank top with beaded edging. "What is there to be anxious about?" I ask myself irritably. But I know. I want to look great tonight, want everyone there to look at me and say, "She can't be seventy-five." It's ridiculous; I hear it all the time, so I know from experience that whatever consolation the words might bring is fleeting. So why do I think it will be different now? I don't think so; it's not my brain that needs these reassurances but my fearful and neurotic heart.

The party is a spectacular success, another of those precious moments when everything comes together just perfectly. Marci and Diane have selected an innovative menu, which the chef, who actually is doing the cooking in Di's very large and well-equipped kitchen, executes superbly. I watch these two women as they perform their hostess roles with such warmth, grace, and pleasure— Di, a beloved friend and companion for more than two decades, and Marci, the daughter with whom I've shared a matchless bond for fifty years. If I ever had any doubt, I know, watching them, that this is not a party given out of duty or obligation; their love, their wish to convey it, is palpable and warms everyone in the room.

They're always beautiful, these two—Di in a lovely gray silk tunic sweater and matching pants, Marci wearing a captivating mauve crushed velvet dress that skims her perfect figure provocatively. Tonight they're also radiant, as if a light has been turned on inside them. It's hard to believe that one is fifty-two, the other fifty. The thought stops me and I wonder, "At what point will we finally replace the internal images of how our parents and grandparents aged with the reality before our eyes?"

I'm happy and excited as I move about the room greeting and being greeted. There are about forty people here; all of them have been an important part of my life for no less than ten years, some as many as thirty. Some old and dear friends are missing: Dorothy, whom I've known for nearly forty years, just had back surgery and can't travel to San Francisco from Alaska, where she lives. Michael, my closest male friend of thirty years—one of the four people to whom I dedicated a book on friendship—is on sabbatical in Paris. The "other Michael" (since he came later, that's how he's often identified in the family) and his wife, Amy, are expecting the birth of their first child any day and can't leave New York. The absence of these three leaves a hole, an empty space where they belong, and it momentarily saddens me to realize that they're not here to share this night.

I know that the ritual encomiums will come after dinner, so I'm not eager for the meal to end. Eventually, however, all have eaten their fill, the table is cleared, coffee is served, and an incredibly beautiful cake is brought forth. It's time. I'm grateful that Marci, who takes over now, has chosen few and well, and I can only hope this isn't going to sound like one of those memorial services where the dead are idealized beyond recognition.

I should have known not to underestimate my friends and their capacity for humor and honesty. Some people have written out what they want to say; others speak spontaneously. Whatever the choice, the tone is the same. One after the other they tell wonderful "Lil" stories that fill the room with knowing laughter, vignettes that speak to a truth about who I am and that capture the essence of each of these relationships and the love we have for each other.

Riese, her voice edged with emotion, talks about the way our friendship has grown, about the great times we've had together. Jim, Diane's husband, who shares with me a technophobic spouse, has everyone laughing with his tales of our electronic bond and the adventures that flow from it. Kim, usually shy about public speaking, takes courage from a new 1920s-style black dress and is hilariously funny as she recounts the story of our friendship through the jackets (yes, jackets) I have given her over the years. Troy, charming, urbane, and always emotionally cautious, talks about the difficulty of staying that way when I'm around. Diane reduces the room to peals of laughter with her story of a shopping expedition in New York that revealed so clearly the conflict between my old poor-girl self and the upper-middle-class person I am now.

I have trouble taking my eyes off the floor as I listen, and I squirm uncomfortably, one shoe scraping at the ground like an awkward child. If I could put my thumb in my mouth it would complete the picture. Yet I'm also thrilled to hear what they say. If I were dead, this would be the perfect memorial service, this coming together of people who love me, not to turn me into a saint but to rejoice in who I am and what I mean to them, with all my foibles and flaws. But I'm alive, not dead, and I'm standing in this room grateful to be able to hear it all—and overwhelmed.

I can't sort out my feelings; it's too much, too fast. By the time Hank and Marci speak I can't take any more in. To this day I have no idea what either of them said. Others tell me they spoke eloquently, movingly, and humorously, but except for hearing Marci's voice saying "my mom" as if she were staking a claim to her specialness, the content eludes me.

When it's over and I've wiped away the tears of joy, those who have written scripts give them to me to keep. I, who am so organized, who rarely loses or misplaces anything, have never found them again.

At home after the party, I'm too full even to talk about it with Hank. I need the solitude of silence that will allow me to process this night, to find a place for it in my heart, to understand all that it means to me. While Hank gets ready for bed, I sit in the living room with the lights out thinking about the events of the evening. "Coming to bed?" he asks.

"No, I need some time to think."

He hugs me and goes off, leaving me to myself. I sit there for about an hour, not really thinking, just feeling the fullness of the night. I'm not ready to let it go, but exhaustion finally overtakes me. I crawl into bed and lie there somewhere between sleeping and waking for what seems like a long time. I don't know if I'm dreaming, but the image of the baby I couldn't dress comes to mind, only now she's fully and appropriately clothed. Is she telling me that I'm on the road to finding the right clothes? It's a nice thought, the perfect end for this wonderful day.

Chapter Twenty-two

I feel as if the last two years have been a rehearsal, as if all the anticipatory angst was necessary to, as we say in the trade, work through
my mother's death and my ascent to the head of the generational
line. After seventy-five years of living and thirty as a therapist, I'm
still awed by the inner workings of the mind, by the way our unconscious can lead the way, if we'll only listen. I know, of course,
that those same unconscious forces can send us down the path of
pain and despair, which is why it's so important to get on speaking
terms with them.

It's two weeks since my birthday party, and I'm surprised that,
as seventy-five settles in on me, I find myself largely untroubled by
it. It's as if the years of wrestling with my fears and feelings, of
chewing on them, spitting them out, and swallowing them again,
allowed me to digest the reality without the emotional bellyache
it gave me before. The old crone of my dreams, her transformation
from a witch to a woman I can recognize and relate to, remains a
recurrent image, a companion in my day life who is also an eloquent reminder of both my fears and their resolution.

Once again I'm struck by the power of this process we call
working through, both by how hard it is when we're in the middle of
it and how magical it seems when we come out on the other side. I
often try to explain it to patients who can't understand what will
enable them to change. But even as the words slip from my
tongue, I know there's no road map that will allow another to see

the route. Until a person has engaged the struggle and won, it remains an abstract therapeutic notion that's hard to grasp. Partly, I suppose, that's because we prefer to believe the movie version that there's some magical insight that will instantly resolve our pain, and partly because psychology itself has helped to foster the view that some restorative "aha" experience awaits us if only we look long and hard enough.

I worry sometimes that this calm inside me is little more than the afterglow of feeling so loved and affirmed by friends and family, that I'll wake up tomorrow or the next day and be back in the struggle. But I don't really think so. It isn't that I believe that this is the end of my contest with getting old. But however that conflict makes itself felt from here on, it will be different because something has shifted inside me and, in some fundamental way, I'm actually glad to be where I am.

Glad to be old? Images of my mother in the last few years of her life rise unbidden to my mind. That's old age, not this—not me with my vibrant, energetic life, with my body that shows the results of years of pushing weights around, with work I love and another lifetime of experiences yet to be lived. It saddens me when I compare my old age to my mother's. Long before she reached seventy-five, she not only looked old, she was old, and her life had been emptied of meaning. She had nothing to do, nowhere to go, no one to count on, not even her children in whom she felt little but the bitter taste of disappointment. She spent the next twenty years waiting for death—wanting it, fearing it, calling upon God to take her to him, while also resisting it with every fiber of her being.

So why don't I feel the triumph that usually comes when I see proof that my life is so different from hers? The word *forgiveness* springs instantly to mind. But I'm not sure I mean it, since I don't think I forgive her, nor do I believe forgiveness is always necessary, or even desirable. Some things are, in fact, unforgivable.

Why, I wonder, does the idea of forgiveness have such a powerful hold on our collective imagination? Probably because the Judeo-Christian tradition, aided by modern psychological theory, exhorts us to forgive, claiming that only forgiveness can ensure resolution. But the insistence on forgiveness as curative can lead us into a miasma of denial as we try to legislate away legitimate feelings in search of those we're told we ought to have. I believe, instead, that in our struggle with the hurts of the past, the quest must be for understanding, which may or may not lead to forgiveness.

I'm not dismissing the possibility or value of forgiveness. My point is simply that forgiveness is not the only path to resolution, and sometimes not even the best one. In my own case, forgiveness seems irrelevant. After a lifetime of trying to come to terms with who my mother was and why we had such a difficult time with each other, I've come to see the complicated web we wove out of the circumstances of our life together. I have no wish to forgive her cruelty or to explain it away. I was the child, she the adult, and the dominant responsibility for making the relationship work was hers, not mine. But that doesn't keep me from understanding that, whatever she did, she didn't do it alone, and that—for reasons of temperament, experience, and who knows what else—neither of us could be for the other what we needed and wanted.

I can't say I wish I could have been the daughter she wanted. I don't. My life would have been poorer in every measure. But I can understand how hard it must have been for her, even how frightening when, from early childhood, I insisted on going my own way and she was forced to confront yet another part of her life that was out of her control. Today, too, I understand far better than ever before how much of her behavior was rooted in an unrecognized depression. And I wonder how different all of our lives might have been if Prozac and its many cousins had been available then. There's sadness in the understanding I have now, but it's no longer tinged with anger—or even regret. Instead it opens the door to compassion for a woman who made her very hard life more bleak and barren that it had to be.

Friends who read this when it was not yet a finished book asked why, given who my mother was, I stuck around in adulthood, why I didn't write this relationship off, why I felt a need to care for her in the final years of her life when she gave me so little.

Questions that reminded me that when she came to visit us six months after Hank and I were married (it was the first time he met her), it didn't take two days before he, too, wondered why I continued to see her. I didn't have a satisfactory answer then, and I don't know if I have one now.

Lest anyone think I'm noble, stupid, or unaccountably caring, however, let me set the record straight. The truth is that, for most of the nearly fifty years that I've lived in California, I did effectively write my mother out of my life. In all that time, she visited me here three times, only once at my express invitation. When I married Hank I didn't invite her to the wedding. I didn't ask myself whether I should or shouldn't; I knew I didn't want her there to ruin the day. And even though I was in New York several times a year, I rarely let her know I was there. On those occasions when I did visit her, which never was more than once a year and often less, our interactions usually were so difficult that, after a few hours, I'd have to hurry off. True, I spoke with her on the phone about once a month, brief conversations that, lest I sometimes forgot, were great reminders of why I didn't see or speak with her more often. But when my brother died and she was left alone at the most vulnerable time of her life, duty asserted itself, prodded no doubt by guilt that lived side by side with some primitive connection that defies words or thought. *She was my mother!*

Not just my mother, but the only parent I had. She, at least, hung around. That's the child's voice, I know, the five-year-old for whom death and desertion are the same. Nevertheless, both child and adult feel some measure of gratitude—the child simply because she was there; the adult also because of the strength and determination she exhibited in the face of a lifetime of trials that would have felled most others. That was her gift to me, not just because she managed to keep us from the orphanage that terrified me so, but because, at a time when girls hardly dreamed of an independent life, she provided for her daughter the model of a woman who, with all its difficulties, could make her way in the world outside the home. I owe her for that, and if there is indeed another world where she now resides, I hope she knows it. But I can know and honor that without the need to forgive the unnecessary anguish she brought to our lives.

I know the downside of aging very well—too well some might say, since that knowledge has, perhaps, made these last years harder than they had to be. Still, it's not just the private angst but the public stigma that makes getting old in America so hard. A fifty-five-year-old man I know, who recently lost his executive job in one of those corporate mergers that are so common today, was smarting over his inability to find an equivalent one. "I sometimes wonder if there's any place in this society for wisdom. I'm a lot smarter today than I was twenty years ago, and I think I'm better at my job now than I was then. But these yo-yo kids who are in charge don't even see me and what I can do; they only see my age, and that's the end of it." A plight common enough to warrant a *New Yorker* cartoon featuring a cigar-smoking, bewildered-looking sixtyish man saying ruefully, "I think I've acquired some wisdom over the years, but there doesn't seem to be much demand for it."

I think about the meaning of those words, about what it will mean in my life when this book is published and I've announced to the world that I'm an old woman. Will my patients see me differently? Will I suddenly become irrelevant, relegated to the nether world of the aged where, like the man in *The New Yorker* cartoon, there will be no demand for my words, my thoughts, my lifetime of accumulated experience and wisdom?

I talk with my friend Riese about my anxieties. "If I publish this book, I'm afraid people who respected me, even sought me out before, will suddenly see me as just another old woman."

She's silent, her dark eyes fixed intently on my face. I can almost hear her internal struggle as she looks for the words to reply honestly. Before she can speak, my anger takes over. "It's an outrage that I should even have to worry about this; that's just the point of the whole drama of aging in this culture, isn't it?"

"That's just what I was thinking," she says. "It is an outrage, and it's also true that you have to be prepared for a range of reactions. This business of aging and the vulnerability that goes with it doesn't lie easily with us, and I expect what you say and how you say it will make some people very uncomfortable. And you know very well that when you puncture their denial, people tend to want to kill the messenger."

"So maybe I shouldn't publish the damn book. Maybe I don't need to open that door and take whatever I'll find on the other side."

She smiles. "That's a lot of maybes, but we both know you'll do it because that's who you are, young or old."

I'm reminded of this conversation a few days later when I'm driving from Berkeley to the city and listening to a National Public Radio (NPR) interview with the author of a book about the aged in America entitled *Another Country*—a title that suggests the depth of isolation, alienation, and fear that afflicts the old of our nation. It's an interesting book, moving and eloquent in its examination of the dilemmas of old age, not just for the old but for the younger generations as well. But when she talks on the air about the social stigma of aging, the best the author can offer is to say that "we need a new language of aging" and suggests, as an example, that we replace words like *old*, *aged*, and *elderly* with the word *elder*.

I understand her point. *Elder* in some cultures is a term of respect, an honorific, an implicit bow to the wisdom embodied in years of living. But among those peoples, it's not the word alone that confers this special status. It's the cultural context within which the word is spoken, the meaning it carries in the society, which, in turn, is related to the role and function the elders fulfill in group life. Among other things, the old in these societies are the carriers of culture and the bearers of their social history. Without them, group life would be immeasurably impoverished and the past would fade out of human memory.

Can we say anything comparable about the elders of our nation? The problem, it seems to me, is not the language but the reality that we live in a society where the old, like the very young, have no social role, no function that adds value to the life of the group. But the young are our future; whatever burden they present carries within it a promise. The old, however, are our past.

And in a society that changes as fast as ours does, where the commonplace of twenty years ago now seems like ancient history, where real historical memory hardly exists, we have little use for the past and those who lived it.

In such a society, changing the word *aged* to *elder* would have as much meaning as it did when we changed *old* to *senior*—a change in the language that has done nothing to ameliorate the stigma of old age. Indeed, nothing will until we are ready to change our deep-seated cultural abhorrence for the aged, which means, among other things, coming to accept our own aging and with it the old people who live among us.

Given the reciprocal and reinforcing interactions between my internal struggles and our national aversion to the aged, it's not a surprise that I've never before been able to glimpse the upside of this stage of life—the sense of accomplishment; the realization that I have nothing more to prove, that I can live as I please and see whom I like; the belief that, in some important ways, I've gained some wisdom; the triumph I feel sometimes when I can stand back and see who I am and what I look like to the world outside; and not least, the inner peace that comes from knowing that I've earned my place in the world and with it, freedom from pressure I've never known before—not just the external pressures but the internal ones that, in the final analysis, are more oppressive and compelling than anything from the outside.

The limitations of time that I confront almost daily remain hard. It's still not the finiteness of my own time that occupies me but the knowledge that there's so little of it left with Hank, or at least with the man I've known and loved for so many wonderful and important years. Not that I think he's going to die soon, but I see the slight mental slippages that I fear signal the beginning of cognitive disarray, which pains me deeply and, in some ways, is worse than contemplating his death. So when friends ask whether we'd like to join them in some plan for next year—whether season tickets to the ballet, a concert series, or a trip abroad—my mind immediately goes to *if*: *if* we're still healthy, *if* we're still around, *if* . . .

It helps that we can talk about all of this, sometimes seriously, often with the kind of ironic, tragicomic humor that's so central to our way of managing the difficulties of living through this stage of our lives. But there's also genuine mirth and joy as we revel in each other and contemplate the sometimes absurd comedy we call *life*.

I know the vision I've presented of getting old is at odds with the sugary one that has become popular in the literature lately. The stories about the seventy-five-year-old woman who runs the Boston marathon in respectable time, the eighty-four-year-old man who plays a hard game of tennis every day, the seventy-year-old woman who's learning to ski, the eighty-one-year-old man who climbs the sheer face of El Capitan in Yosemite, the hundred-and-two-year-old woman who graduates from high school with a 4.0 grade point, the ninety-year-old man who still has an eye for the women and the wherewithal to do something about it—all these are wonderfully inspiring. But how many of us can aspire to such achievements? How many of us want to?

This isn't to say that these remarkable feats aren't an important part of the modern aging narrative. As we continue to live longer, healthier lives more of us will find physical and mental capacities unknown in the elders of earlier times. Meanwhile, just knowing such people exist is helpful, since they provide models of the possible, not just for those of us who are already old but, more important, for our children who are not far behind.

The other side of these rah-rah efforts to cheer ourselves up, however, is that they set us up for false expectations that can leave us more depressed than facing the truth in all its complexity. Betty Friedan's insistence in *The Fountain of Age* that getting old is just a state of mind—that the seventies and eighties are a breeze so long as we find the secret to what she calls *vital aging*—is a lovely but unreal fantasy. And William Regelson's *The Superhormone Promise*, which declares that aging is "not a normal life event but a disease," is surely the ultimate denial.

Certainly, if we can find the key to living vital, engaged, and productive lives into old age these years will be easier. But until this life stage, that engagement has been found in the expectations and institutions by which our lives were bound—family, school, work. When our schooling is done, our families no longer need us, and the world of work closes its doors, whether at our instigation or theirs, then what? Without the institutions to give shape and meaning to our daily lives, we're set adrift into uncharted territory. True, some people find their way. They go to school, they climb mountains, they volunteer for much needed public service. But this, by and large, is a gift of the privileged—those of us who have the good health and the financial resources to make such a life possible.

For all of us, however—whether rich or poor, healthy or infirm— getting old is fraught with inescapable irony. At the very moment when we have time, we're intensely aware of how little of it is left. At the very time when we feel wise, few want to hear what we have to say. At the very season when we're ready to fly, we're hobbled by a body that keeps us grounded.

Faced with these contradictory realities, we're forced to reorder our image of ourselves, a redefinition of self and life that infuses these years with the sadness that comes with loss. And that's another inalienable fact: Old age, whatever else we may say about its positives and negatives, inescapably confronts us with a keen sense of loss—the loss of roles, of friends and loved ones, of the structure and clarity of our lives until now, of the physical capabilities that just yesterday we took for granted.

It may be momentarily comforting to some people to read that the lumps, bumps, thinning hair, waning strength, and memory lapses that come with age don't count, that the assault to the self that accompanies these changes is just vanity, an unnecessary product of our narcissism. But the reassurance is fleeting, and the comfort slips away quickly when we come up against our waning powers. Not just the serious ones, but the small daily reminders that we can no longer count on our bodies to do what we ask of them.

Personally, when I hear the cheery platitudes about the joys of getting old I want to shout: "Oh yeah! Tell it to my brain when it has trouble getting perfectly ordinary words to my tongue. Or to my body when it huffs and puffs up a hill it climbed easily just a couple of years ago. Or to my drooping belly that no longer responds to the crunches that used to keep it in shape."

When I stare these truths in the face, it's hard sometimes not to think, "Okay, so even if seventy-five is fine, seventy-six is coming, and seventy-seven, and seventy-eight, and . . . As inevitably as the sun will rise, the day will come when there's nothing but decline and death left."

That's true, of course, but it's not the whole truth.

Then I remember that this is what I thought when seventy-five was still on the horizon and that now that I'm actually living it the fears have faded before the reality of a life that's no different than it was before, except that each day seems more precious to me now. Which may mean only that this is the central dilemma of this time of life—an intense appreciation of the moment that lives side by side with the knowledge that it's fleeting, a paradox that brings a sharp poignancy to the beauty and pain in every experience, along with a wish to hold on, while knowing we have no choice but to let go. It's not an easy lesson to learn, but it's the one we need if we're to make our way relatively peacefully through the tangle of sorrow and joy that old age brings.

A C K N O W L E D G M E N T S

No book, not even such a personal story as this, is ever written without the background support of others. For their part as readers of the manuscript in process, I owe thanks to Judith Barnard, Diane Ehrensaft, Ruth Goldman, Rosanna Hertz, Anita Hill, Dorothy Jones, Michael Kimmel, Michael Krasny, Walker Meade, Michael Rogin, and Terry Stein. Together, they made this a better, stronger work.

To Kim Chernin, a special loving word of gratitude for her yeoman duty in helping bring this book to life. From the first word to the last she stood by—reading, commenting, encouraging, keeping the faith when I faltered, and urging me on at every step of the way.

To Rhoda Weyr, my agent through ten books and more than a quarter of a century, I can only say, "It's been a great ride."

Thanks, also, to Helene Atwan, the director of Beacon Press and the very wise editor of this book. It has been a pleasure.

And then, of course, there's my family, without whom my whole life wouldn't be possible: my daughter, Marci, and her partner, Larry; my grandson, Blake, and our newest member, his soon-to-be wife, Margaret; and last but never least, my husband, Hank. Thank you all just for being.